D0996627

VALENTINO ROSSI

PORTRAIT OF A MotoGENIUS

First published July 2005
Reprinted September 2005

A catalogue record for this book is available from the British Library

ISBN 1 84425 236 1

Library of Congress catalog card no. 2005926139

Published by Haynes Publishing, Sparkford, Yeovil, Somerset BA22 7JJ, UK
Tel: +44 (0)1963 442030
Fax: +44 (0)1963 440001
E-mail: sales@haynes.co.uk
Website: www.haynes.co.uk

Haynes North America, Inc., 861 Lawrence Drive, Newbury Park, California 91320, USA

Designed by Lee Parsons

Printed and bound in England by J. H. Haynes & Co. Ltd, Sparkford

Dedication:

To Debs

ACKNOWLEDGEMENTS

With special thanks to: Giacomo Agostini, Gibo Badioli, Katie Baines, Paul Barshon, Mathew Birt, Axle Briggs, Jeremy Burgess, Gary Coleman, Ercole Colombo, Mick Doohan, Alison Forth, Peter Fox, Fermino Fraternali, David Goldman, Patrick Gosling, Charlie Green, Marco Guidetti, Henk Keulemans, Eddie Lawson, Debs Leigh, Phil Long, Michele Lupi, Patrik Lundin, Rossana Marelli (AGV Italy), John Mockett, Ken Nemoto, Andy Pope, Rupert Paul, Carlo Pernat, Michael Scott, Gigi Soldano, Dr Martin Raines, King Kenny Roberts, Graziano Rossi, Stefania Rossi, Valentino Rossi, Michel Turco, Joan Turner, Claudio Vitale and many more

VALENTINO

ROSSI

PORTRAIT OF A MotoGENIUS

Mat Oxley

Haynes Publishing

Contents

8 BEING VALENTINO

26 HAIR ROSSI

28 VICTORY VALENTINO

34 ROSSI POSSE

40 ROSSI LIDS

44 ROSSI RELIGION

50 GROWING UP FAST

66 125s

78 250s

88 500s

100 **MOTOGP HONDA**

110 **MOTOGP YAMAHA**

126 **PAPA ROSSI**

130 **METAL ROSSI**

142 **ROSSI RIVALS**

146 **ROSSI DOWN**

152 **ROSSI VERSUS HISTORY**

154 **AUTO ROSSI**

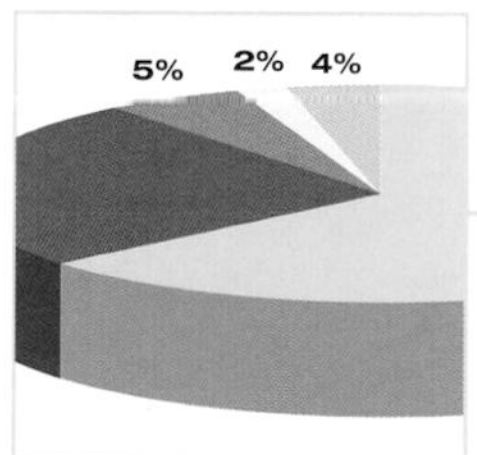

156 **ROSSI BY NUMBERS**

158 **SPROCKET ROSSI**

Valentino Rossi is probably the fastest and certainly the most famous motorcycle racer who has ever walked this planet. He has won a pile of world titles and wooed millions of fans with his magical ability to wring the maximum out of an engine and a pair of wheels.

He's the petrolhead who became a pop star, hopelessly addicted to speed and irresistible to fans of all shapes and sizes: bikers and non-bikers, guys and girls, young and old. He earns his living from a violent and risky business, laying his life on the line, week in, week out, usually looking like he's really just having a bit of a laugh.

Motorsport in the 21st century is very much a science, a slave to the overbearing laws of physics, a digital duel of zeroes and ones. And yet Valentino races with an old-school cavalier swagger, his extraordinary natural ability allowing him to do things with a 210mph motorcycle that would take any normal human being deep into the disaster zone. Watching him at the height of his powers is special – he's totally at one with his motorcycle, melding muscle and metal into a seamless whole, a unique union of man and machine.

We're lucky to be witnessing a remarkable moment in bike racing history. As Carlo Pernat – the man who gave Vale his big break ten years ago – puts it: 'A rider like Valentino is born every 20 years. For me he's similar to guys like Pele, McEnroe, Muhammad Ali or Maradona, people who tower over their sports.' Pernat isn't wrong, Valentino's shadow casts right across motorcycle racing, so that he's almost bigger than the sport itself.

Off the bike he's equally outstanding, with a lust for life that burns so brightly and a rock 'n' roll attitude that distinguishes him from so many of today's ass-kissing sports stars. Valentino is one of those rare people who every day extracts the maximum out of life, but he always gives as good as he gets…

Mat Oxley

London

July 2005

MILAGRO

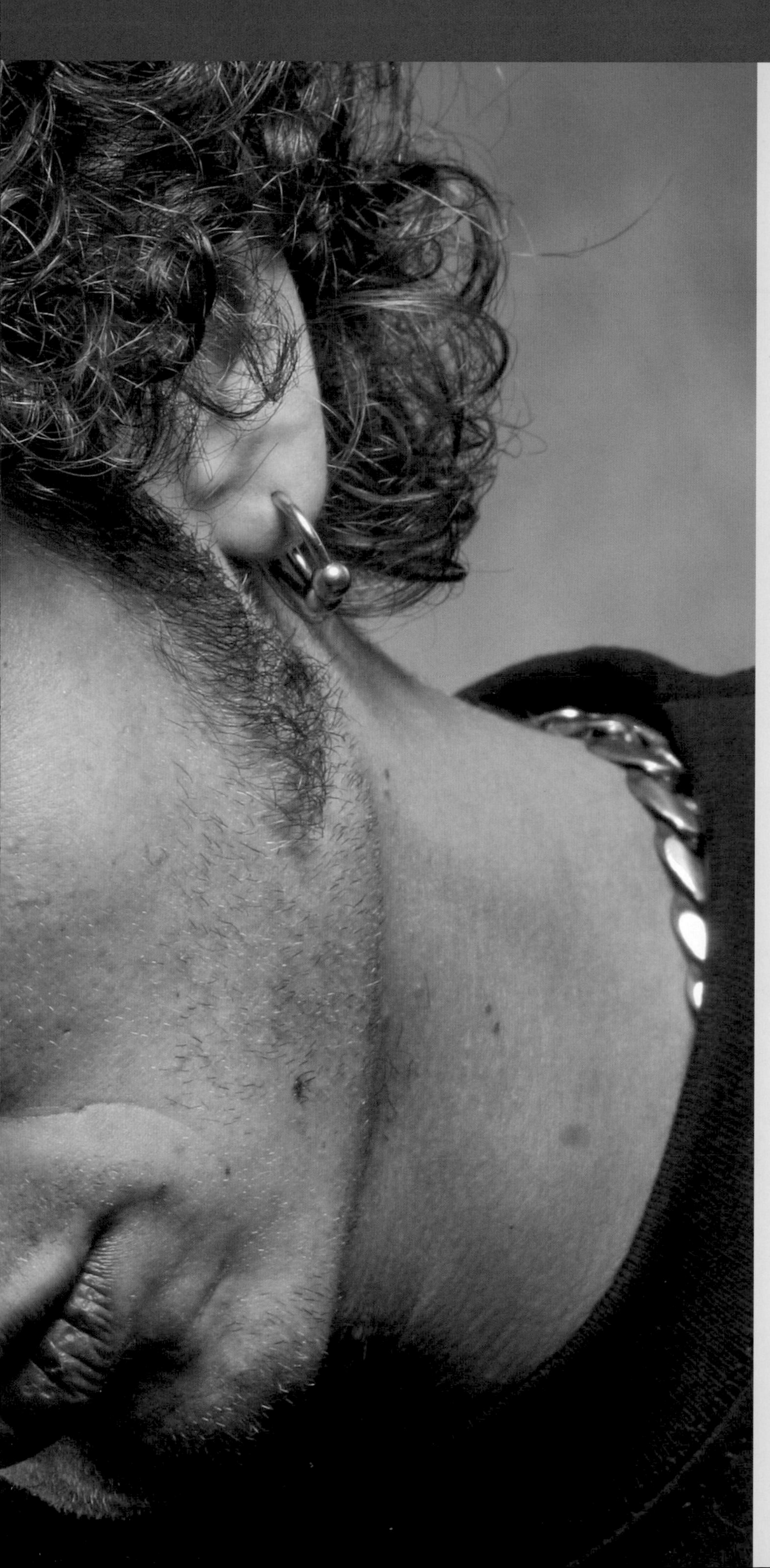

BEING VALENTINO

It's not just about being fast...

Valentino Rossi is a fan of the late Steve McQueen. There are obvious parallels between the lives of the World Champion bike racer and the uber-cool Hollywood actor. Valentino likes to live fast and loose, just like McQueen did. He's addicted to speed, just like McQueen was. He parties hard, just like McQueen did. His career is driven by an appetite for fun and revenge, just like McQueen's was. And he has that same conviction of greatness, that same unflinching self-confidence of someone who knows he's really good, just like McQueen had.

McQueen was an accomplished dirt bike racer, good enough to race for the USA's world enduro team. Quite simply, he lived for speed, just like Valentino does. 'All the racers I know race because it's something that's inside of them,' McQueen said. 'They're not courting death. They're courting being alive.' McQueen had a term for guys he ▶

◀ It's a tough life, this GP racing. Valentino on holiday in Tunisia in '98. The big grin belies a troubled soul – he was midway through his first 250 season, crashing too much and getting eaten alive by the Italian media.
MILAGRO

▶ really respected – 'he's full of juice,' he'd say – and he would certainly have appreciated the fact that Valentino is so full of juice he bubbles over, with enough of the stuff to touch the lives of millions. He radiates a lust for life that most human beings can't help falling for, just like McQueen did back in the '60s and '70s.

Of course, there are contrasts between these two gods of speed and cool. McQueen spent most of his life acting or playing the fool and the rest of his time racing motorcycles. Rossi spends most of his life racing bikes and the rest of the time acting up or playing the fool. But had they been able to spend time together they would've perfectly understood each other. They would've spent their days thrashing around on dirt bikes, getting into deep discussions about tyre compounds and suspension settings, and their nights getting drunk and talking nonsense. Because that's what being Valentino is all about: race hard, play hard.

He's certainly no longer the impish boy racer who had a smile for everyone, even his most belligerent 125 and 250 rivals. These days he's a grown man in a tough world, and perhaps the McQueen fetish is all about growing up. Look at Valentino now, he's no more the playful kid with the trance cadet hairdo, he's gone all rugged, unkempt and unshaven, like a grown-up who's got better things to worry about than preening and polishing. And on the track he's no longer boy wonder, he's a heavyweight fighter. That vicious clash with arch-rival Gibernau at the 2005 Spanish GP proved that.

But people who balk at this more macho Valentino should remember that he competes in one of the cruellest, most vicious sports – a world of corporate overkill in the paddock and sudden death on the racetrack. It's not the kind of world you pass through without making enemies, and if you can use your enemies for motivation, then why not?

Like McQueen, Valentino is one of those people who always gets the maximum out of life. And like Vale, McQueen was good at making enemies. McQueen was also well-known for taking risky roles at the height of his commercial powers, just like Valentino. Vale loves laying it on the line, taking risks, because he's courting being alive. Someone once said of McQueen: 'He didn't die wondering.' Neither will Valentino… ■

◀ The king indeed. Italian *Rolling Stone* dressed Valentino like Elvis and put him on its cover in December 2003. Editor Michele Lupi is a mate of Vale's and spends much time trying to educate the youngster in the ways of the rock 'n' roll lifestyle.
ROLLING STONE

'Racing is life, the rest is just waiting'

Steve McQueen,
Le Mans 1971

Valentino waiting to race, Rio, July 2004. On this day he needn't have bothered – he ended up crashing out. MILAGRO

YAMAHA
YAMAHA
YAMAHA

Valentino hasn't had a steady girlfriend for a while. And he hardly ever brings girls to races. They appear occasionally but never for very long – he seems to be enjoying the young, free, single lifestyle. 'When you make this life is very difficult to have a girl,' he says. 'If you bring her to a GP maybe she's bored, so I stay alone at races, is better. Then when you stay one week at a racetrack, you come back home and you have some power to use, you need to have fun, go out with friends, go to the disco, but your girlfriend has just stayed one week doing all this, so when I come home, she say 'can we see a movie?'. So is difficult.'

Not that that has stopped him from enjoying the attentions of the gentler sex. 'We really enjoy having so many girls around!' says Vale's best mate Uccio. 'Maybe some top riders or superstars worry "is this girl coming to see me because I'm famous or does she really like me?", but Valentino doesn't think like that, he always says "I don't care why she's coming to see me, I'm just happy that she's coming".'

Former Aprilia GP boss Carlo Pernat has always been amazed at Vale's ways with the ladies. 'I've never seen so many girls around a rider, maybe Sheene or

▲ The Valenteenyboppers go nuts at Mugello '98. He was only just beginning to get used to all the fuss.
MILAGRO

► You wouldn't find many macho bike racers happy to hang out with a tranny. Vale sharing a laugh with notorious Italian DJ Platinette at Imola 1999.
MILAGRO

Lucchinelli (hard-partying premier-class stars of the '70s and '80s) but never so many,' he says. 'Valentino doesn't like to stay with a girl more than two or three months. He lived like a kid then and he lives like a kid now, with the same friends, the same way of life. After the racing is finished it's impossible to find him, no-one knows where he goes, maybe he's in London, maybe he's in a disco with some friends he's known since he was a boy. He never changes, he doesn't want to be famous, he doesn't want a movie-star girlfriend, he doesn't want to be in the papers with famous people.'

▲Who's that girl? Valentino keeps his private life private, but this mystery lady turned up to spend some time with him at Le Mans 2004.

GOLD AND GOOSE

▲ Breakfast of a champion, breaking his fast with half-brother Luca at mum's house in Tavullia. This is where he goes to escape the stresses of his high-speed life.
VITALE

► Vale never takes himself too seriously, which is why his personal logo is a super-slow tortoise. He has a sticker of the tortoise on the yokes of his M1 and a tattoo on his belly.
GOLD AND GOOSE

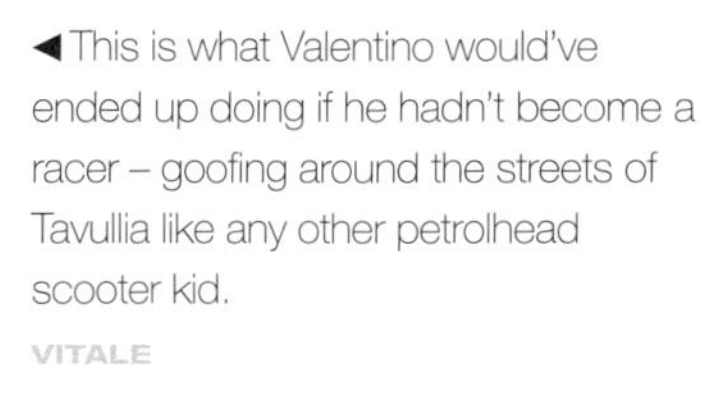

◀ This is what Valentino would've ended up doing if he hadn't become a racer – goofing around the streets of Tavullia like any other petrolhead scooter kid.

VITALE

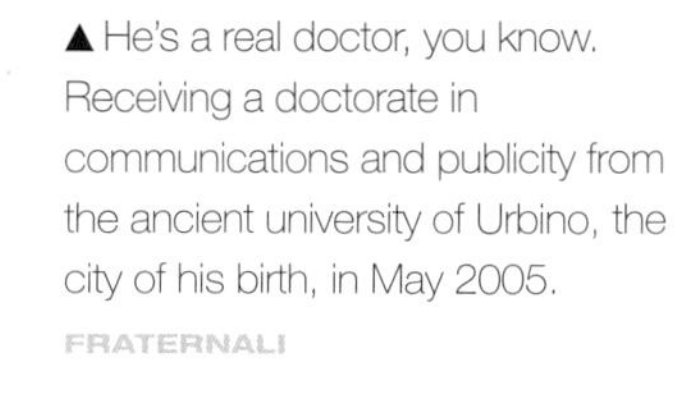

▲ He's a real doctor, you know. Receiving a doctorate in communications and publicity from the ancient university of Urbino, the city of his birth, in May 2005.

FRATERNALI

Touch and ye shall be touched. The Yamaha crew pay homage after Valentino's runaway win at Estoril, 2004. This was the victory that started the final push to his greatest world title success. Note white-haired manager Gibo and best mate Uccio, with yellow visor.

MILAGRO

46
MOTUL

▲ You could never say 21st century Valentino isn't cool. But he definitely didn't used to be. Funny, yes, daft, definitely, charming, sure, but cool? Nah.

MILAGRO

► A good yawn introduces extra oxygen to the system, which is why some racers yawn like crazy while waiting on the grid, even though they're most definitely not bored. But this is Valentino being bored…

MILAGRO

◄ In the spring of 2003, with the US/UK invasion of Iraq ready to roll, most MotoGP riders kept quiet about the coming carnage, perhaps wary they might upset a corporate sponsor or two. Not Valentino. He was loud and proud on the issue: 'Peace – make love, not war' was the message.

MILAGRO

► If he were a teenager now, he'd wear a hoodie and be the proud owner of an ASBO.
VITALE

► A word in your shell-like. Graziano gives his boy some sensible advice.
VITALE

◀ The Tavullia tobacconist – like most of Tavullia – is a shrine to Valentino and his achievements.
VITALE

◀ 'Hello, is that the Tavullia council graffiti unit? Some kids have made a real mess of this wall in the town square.'
VITALE

'Very decisive man, great hands, full of personality'

Palmist Joan Elizabeth

Palmist Joan Elizabeth read Vale's hands, knowing only that they belonged to a bike racer, nothing more. 'His past lifeline curves round the base of the thumb. Nothing to do with longevity; it's how a person lives their life. This chap is very independent. Childhood may not have been an easy time. It's not a criticism of parenting; his very strong, independent spirit made him someone who wasn't easy to parent. It seems his life has gone in blocks, with some difficulties.

'He's unsure – not from his lack of commitment but other people's. With that sorted I see him zooming into the future in a controlled way; this chap has control over his life. Something of a temper I'd suggest, but he's probably only lost it once or twice because he likes to be in control.

'I know he's a racer but I have to say I'm surprised. It's almost as if he got into what he's doing by default. I'd assumed that, because of the strong determination in his hands, he'd be very clear about what he's doing. In fact there seems to be a sort of vagueness. He probably found that he was very gifted and thought "I'll have a go". One day he'll wake up and say "I've had enough of this", and do something completely different. It'll certainly be creative. He's a very intelligent chap who could choose any career.

'Whatever he does needs movement, people, changes. Repetition is like death to him. A very emotional man too; his heart line shows more than his share of emotional events, some of which he's vowed never to repeat. He's built a strong defensive mechanism around him.

'He has a very sympathetic nature, but he likes to get on with it. Money-wise there's strong financial security. He's a very intuitive man who sums up people quickly. He doesn't suffer fools gladly. I wouldn't like to get on the wrong side of him. He may have a lot of acquaintances but very few real friends. If he makes a friend, that's it, you've got him for life.'

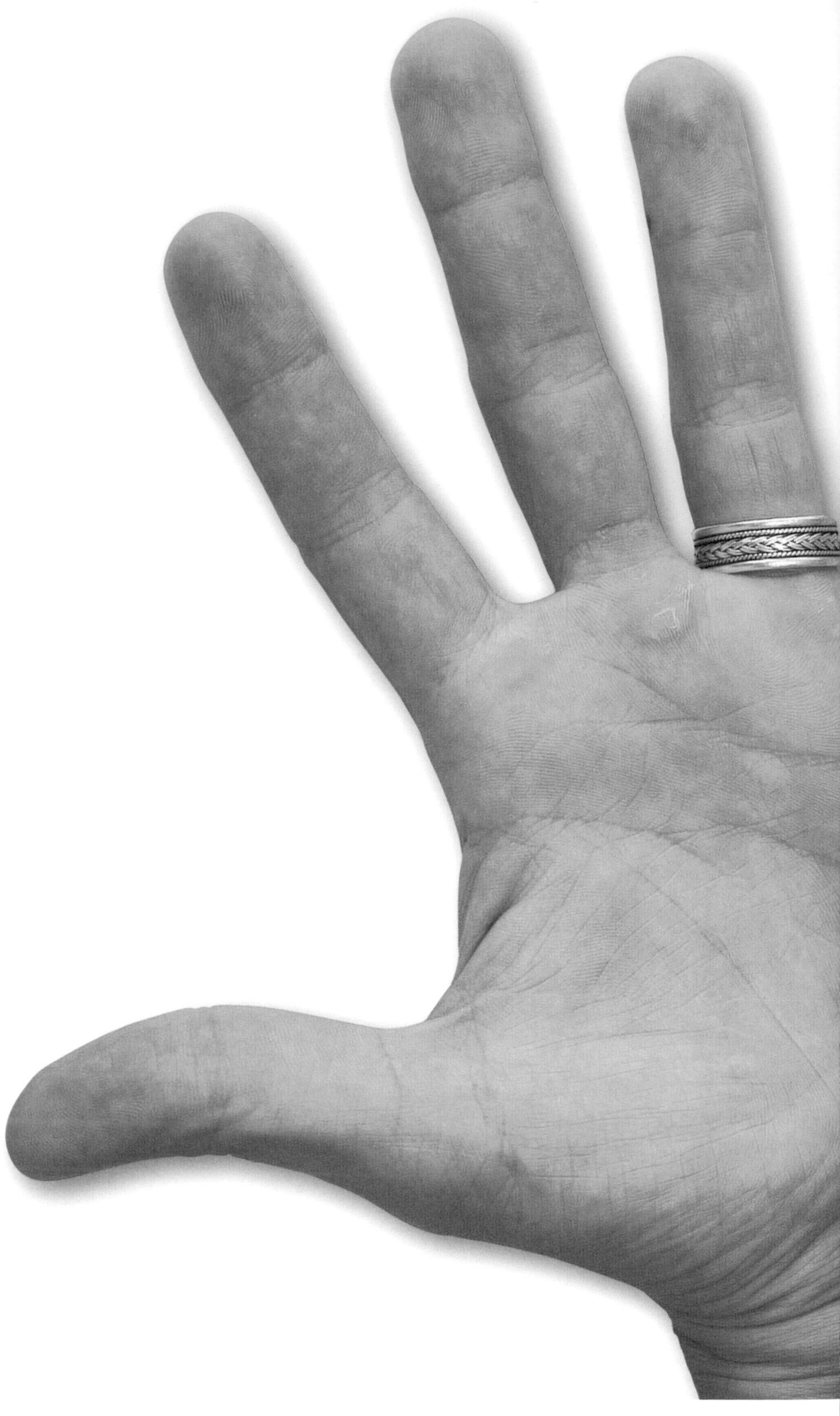

These are the hands of the master – the parts of Valentino's body that interact between his amazing racing brain and his motorcycle. They're not the gnarled hands of some veteran GP campaigners and they're not the hands of a builder, all sausage fingers and podgy palms. If anything, they're the hands of an artist, which fits Rossi's highly graceful style of riding.

Most interesting of all, Vale is left-handed. Left-handed people are said to use their brains differently from the majority; for example, they're supposed to benefit from greater integration of both brain hemispheres in processing information. They're also supposed to be more creative, which might explain Rossi's ability to

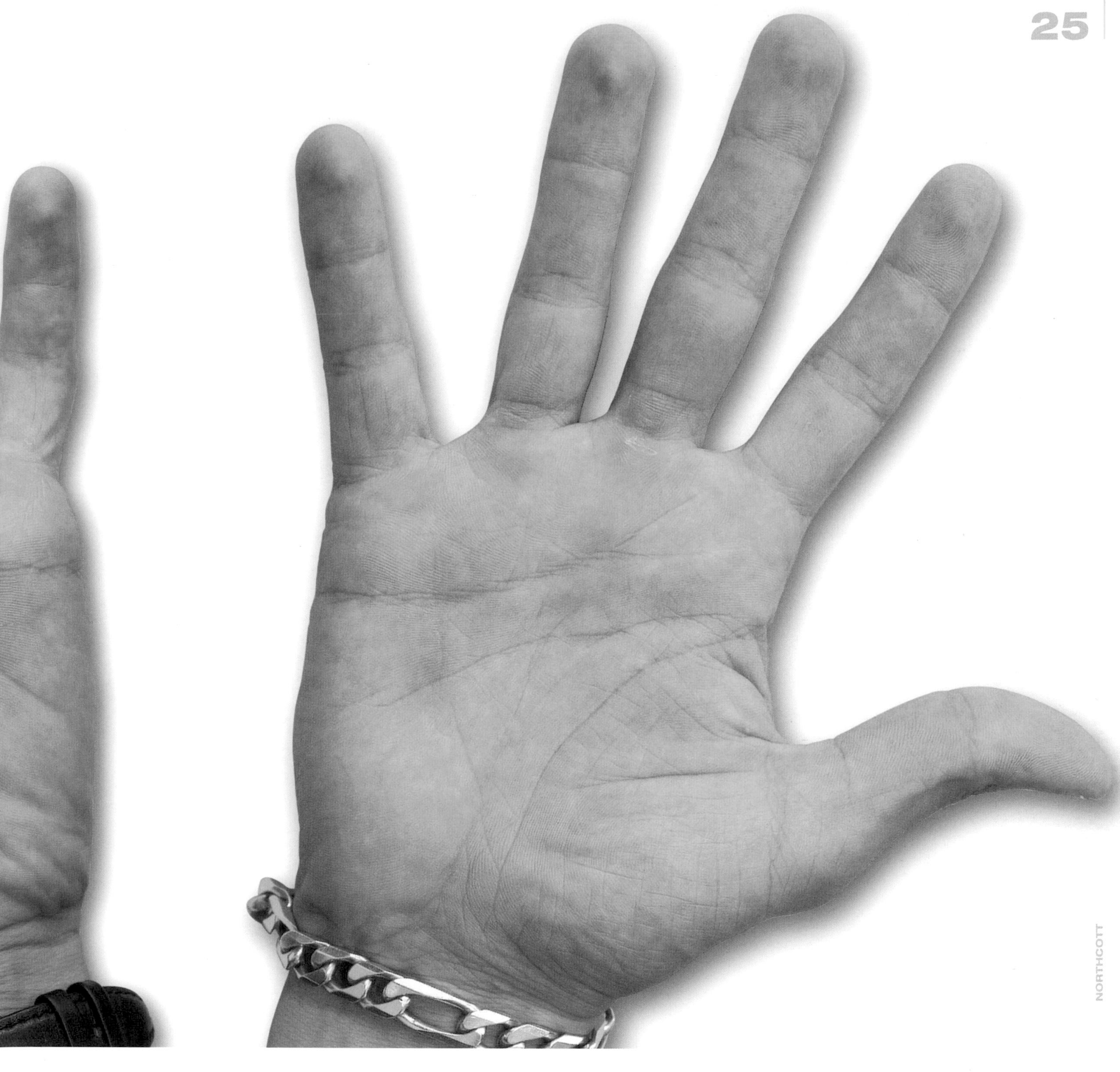
NORTHCOTT

conjure up unusual racing lines that few rivals seem able to attempt. He's in good company here – football legend Pele is left-handed, and so were F1 racer Ayrton Senna, Jimi Hendrix, Napoleon and Michelangelo.

So far (touch wood) Valentino has been pretty lucky injury-wise, so his hands aren't as wrecked as those belonging to many motorcycle racers. He's one of those riders with an apparent ability to bounce, tumble and roll without incurring major physical damage. Some riders are like that and no-one is really sure why – is it an innate talent to crash well, or do these riders have stronger bones and more flexible joints than other less fortunate riders?

But his hands have suffered somewhat in his dozen years of minimoto and Grand Prix racing. The little finger on his left hand is a bit of a mess. He broke the digit when he crashed out of a 125 European championship race at Assen in 1995 and the lower two bones have since fused together, leaving a nasty, crooked pinkie. 'I crash very much in '95 and '96, maybe 20 times.'

And Valentino's hands do suffer from the day-to-day rigours of high-speed motorcycle racing. The tops of his palms are hard and calloused, like the soles of a barefoot walker's feet, from gripping the handlebars like his life depends on it (which it does, of course).

‘I saw a girl in Ibiza last week with dyed red hair, it looked cool, so I went for the same’

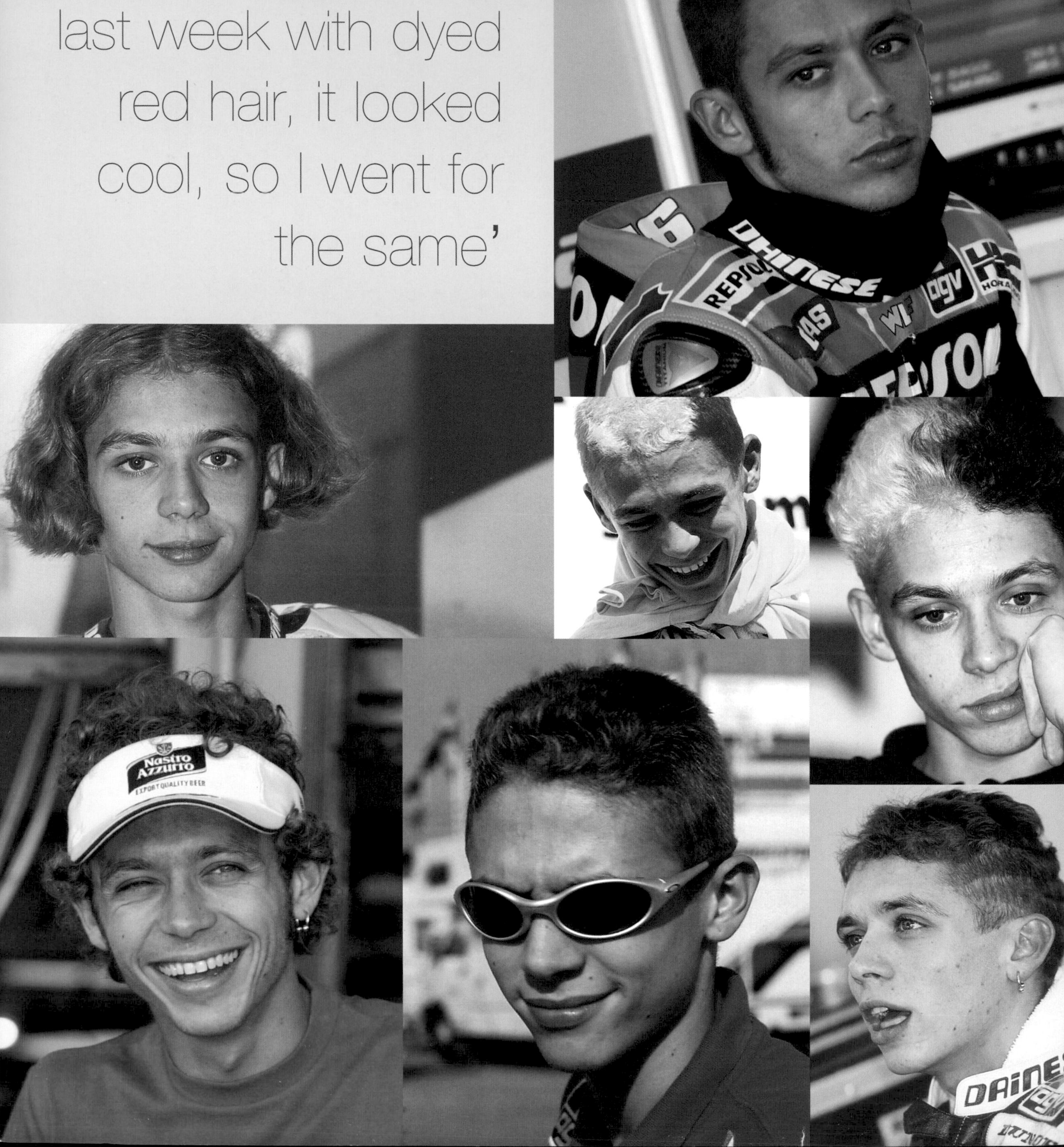

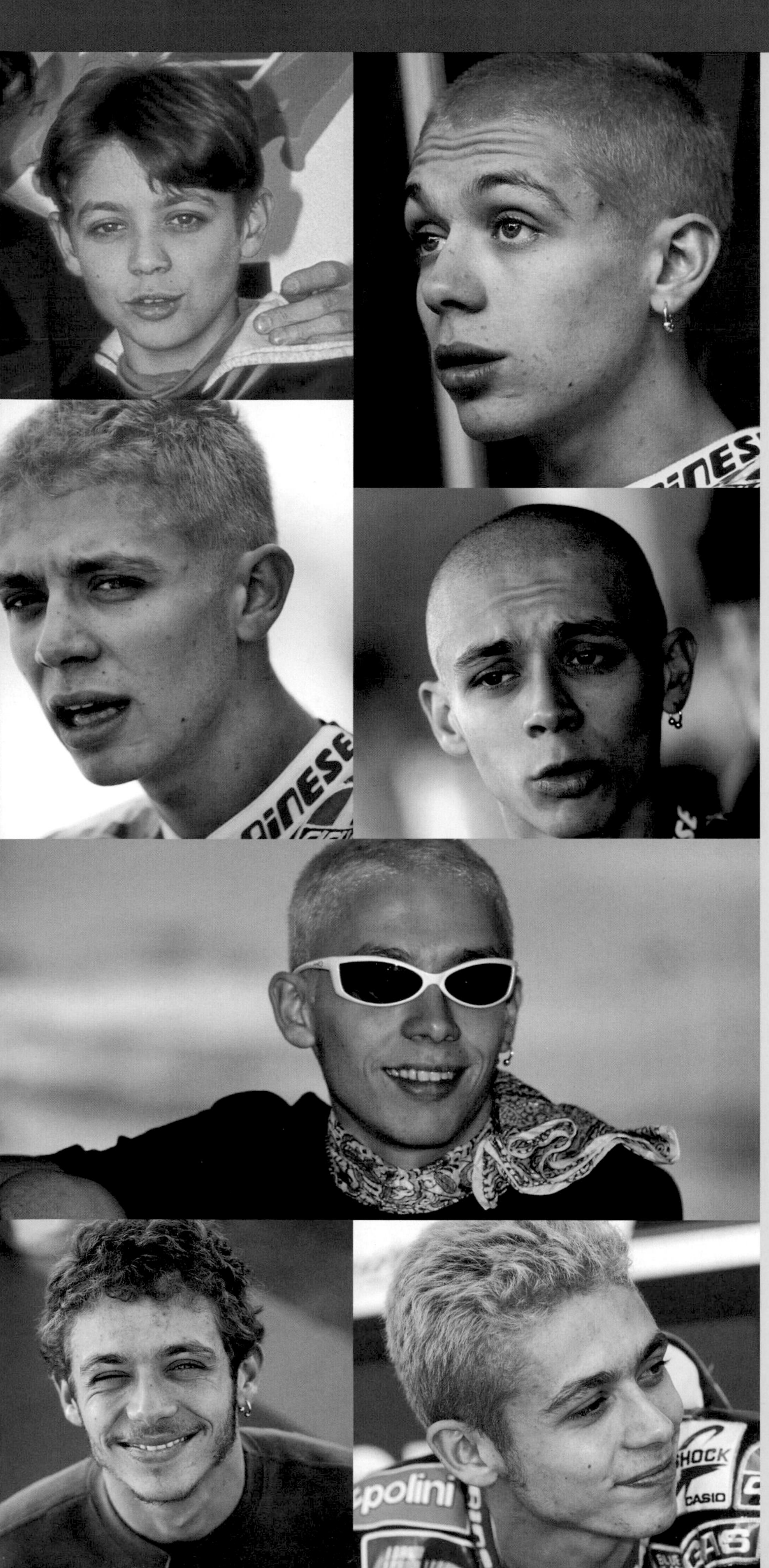

HAIR ROSSI

Vale's dozen years of cool and not so cool coiffures

Valentino is a master of the makeover, a one-man boom for the hairdressing industry. His tonsorial adventures have veered this way and that, from red to green, from blue to orange, from black and white to red, white and green. But what do they tell us about the man? Does each hairdo suggest the ever-changing moods of a mercurial spirit? Nah, they all tell us the same thing – that the man likes a laugh and that he doesn't want to be taken too seriously.

Photos:
GOLD AND GOOSE, KEULEMANS

46
agv
RINGO
DAINESE
Nastro
Azzurro
alpinestars
domino
polini
aprilia
46
agv
polini
Nastro
Azzurro
aprilia
DUNLOP

VICTORY VALENTINO

Victory always means one thing for Vale – party time

The Mad Hatter and the crazy little 125 rider get the party started at Brno '97. Vale has just won his first world title and what better way to celebrate than by strapping a giant *numero uno* to his back. Note Uccio with shades on head.

GOLD AND GOOSE

▼ Valentino had the Jerez crowd in hysterics after he'd won the '99 Spanish 250 GP. Halfway around his victory lap he parked his Aprilia and disappeared into this Portaloo.

GOLD AND GOOSE

Valentino's wacky victory celebrations won him tens of thousands of fans long before his riding genius became fully apparent to the world. Right from the start in '97, Vale, Uccio and their mates put serious effort into their post-race pranks.

Uccio: 'I was one of ten people who would meet on Tuesdays before races to organise the gag. Then I would arrive at the track on Wednesdays to find a nice place to do the gag. We bought the plastic sheeting for the 'Superfumi' cape and made it ourselves for Assen '97. At Mugello that year Valentino rode his victory lap with a blow-up doll. We had that idea at Mugello, so we rang someone from the fan club to buy a blow-up doll from a sex shop!'

Vale: 'The gags are just a game, just some fun with the people in my fan club. The ideas usually came to us in a bar in Tavullia at two in the morning.'

Graziano: 'Valentino's victory gags aren't so much for the fans, they're more for his friends and the fan club, they're important to improve his relationship with the people who are behind him, the people who love him. The gags show that he's very different from other riders. My favourite was Jerez in '99, when he stopped on the victory lap and went into a marshal's toilet.'

► 'Sorry mate, it may be a little too late for a urine sample.' Goggle-eyed on champagne, Vale gives the Aussie GP official the bad news. Phillip Island will probably never forget the party that followed his 2004 title-winning ride.

MILAGRO

▼ 'Who do you think you are, son, Valentino Rossi?' Vale's fan club, dressed as Italian speed cops, nick their hero after he'd won the 2002 Italian GP. And he'd only been doing 210mph down the start-finish.

MILAGRO

▲ Valentino reckoned the media gave him such a hard time after a run of mediocre results during 2003 that they'd put him on the chain gang. Czech GP victory gave him his jailbreak.

MILAGRO

▼ Vale donned this cape after winning the '97 Dutch 125 GP. The Superfumi tag came from his first racing nickname, Rossifumi, which came from Japanese GP star Norifumi Abe. Got that?

GOLD AND GOOSE

► Smoking is bad for your health but the people love it anyway. Vale gets another rolling burn-out started at the Sachsenring.

GOLD AND GOOSE

◀ It's 2002 and Brazil has just won the world cup in Japan. Meanwhile in Rio, Vale has just won the MotoGP world title. Cue some wild football-style celebrations.
GOLD AND GOOSE

▲ One week after getting relegated to the back of the grid for scrubbing clean his grid slot at Doha 2004, Vale had the last laugh in Malaysia. In every sense, he wiped the floor…
MILAGRO

▲ 'What's my number?' Just in case anyone wasn't already sure, Vale and his coterie remind the masses after winning the 1998 Imola 250 GP.
GOLD AND GOOSE

GAULOISES
YAMAHA
GAULOISES
YAMAHA
DAINESE
GAULOISES
YAMAHA
Rossi
agv
GAULOISES
YAMAHA
MOTUL
MICHELIN

The man with a plan. Vale and his crew at Sepang, winter tests, November 2004 (left to right): Brent Stephens, Alex Briggs, Matteo Flamigni, JB, Vale, Bernard Ansiau, team boss Davide Brivio, Gary Coleman.

GOLD AND GOOSE

ROSSI POSSE

The people who help make Valentino great

'As a guy to work for, you'd struggle to find someone better. If anything goes wrong with the bike he doesn't hold grudges with anyone, he knows that's just racing. He always puts more emphasis on the race side of things – watch how many laps he does on race set-up and race tyres during practice.'

Brent Stephens, mechanic

'Big-head syndrome hasn't come into his life, not as far as I can see, anyway, I think his mates keep him straight there. He's great because he never gives up and he's very apologetic if he doesn't win. Downsides? He's got too many fans, so it's bloody hard to get in and out of the garage!'

Gary Coleman, pit assistant

'He never says a bad word and he never complains. He's a lot of fun, a nice person to work with – which is sometimes surprising because some riders aren't so nice.'

Bernard Ansiau, mechanic

'We have been friends since we were five. We used to race each other on minimotos, but I stopped after that and started going to races with him. I always knew he was very fast but I never imagined the future, we were too young to notice that he might be a really good rider. In '96 and '97 I was amazed at what was happening. We had never imagined how big our adventure would become, but I was very happy that Valentino realised his dream. To this day our relationship has never changed, but he has changed in the way he relates to the media, the fans, the people who aren't around him all the time.'

Uccio Salucci, best mate and right-hand man

▼ Thick as thieves since they were five: Valentino and Uccio.

GOLD AND GOOSE

'I'm very happy for him. My own feeling is more joy than pride, I'm not a proud person. Every time he achieves another success it's a pleasurable surprise but I will always remember him winning the 125 title in '97. We shared this camper all summer and we were always fighting. It was terrible because he cannot go to bed before one o'clock, it's impossible for him, then I had to wake him up in the morning… the most difficult job in the world! I had to wake him once, twice, three times. In the end I had to get his engineer to do it.'

Graziano Rossi, father

◀ She brought him up well – Vale celebrates his 2004 title with mum and half-brother Luca.

MILAGRO

'The thing I really like about him is the personal stuff. If I had to tell you what's his best quality, it wouldn't be his riding talent.'

Stefania Rossi, mother

▼ Ahhhh… Valentino and his dad have always been close.

MILAGRO

'Ask most race mechanics what they think of their riders and a lot of them will say they're pricks, but Valentino's a great person. Within the first week of knowing him, he knew about me, about my family, he knew all of that. And he just loves all kinds of racing: bikes, rallying, F1, anything to do with engines. Watch some rallying on TV with him and he squeals with delight watching a car get sideways through a corner, he just loves it all.'

Alex 'Axle' Briggs, mechanic

▼ Vale and Axle spend their winters performing in front of empty grandstands – MotoGP's not-so-glamorous side.

GOLD AND GOOSE

► 'Then she said...' Vale amuses JB, Uccio and Matteo during a lull in winter testing, Phillip Island, January 2005.

GOLD AND GOOSE

'He has the mental capacity to take on board more than the other guys'

Jeremy Burgess

'He has better application and better understanding than any other rider I've worked with. And he has the mental capacity to take on board a lot more than perhaps other guys out there, so he's got the confidence in himself and in us to get the bike right leading into a race, when most riders are reluctant to make changes to the set-up.'
Jeremy Burgess, crew chief

'It's interesting to see how he rides in different conditions. When the bike isn't 100 per cent he modifies his riding style to get the best out of it. The data shows us how he uses the brake and throttle differently, how he uses different lines to make the best of any situation. He's always very logical in the pits, so he's easy to work with.'
Matteo Flamigni, data technician

▲ Getting to the heart of the matter – Valentino, JB and Matteo discuss set-up options at the 2004 German GP.
BARSHON

1997 – 125 WORLD CHAMPIONSHIP

◀ Things always used to seem more simple – this lid is straightforward by Vale's standards: sun and moon with the red, white and green of the Italian flag. All Vale's helmet designs are done by graphic designer Aldo Drudi, an old mate of Graziano's.

PEACE & LOVE – 1999 ITALIAN GP

▼▶ Valentino adopted a Peace & Love theme for his ride in the 1999 250 Italian GP. Turquoise inlaid into his usual sun and moon theme, along with a CND peace logo and his alter ego Valentinik firing flowers from a laser gun.

2001 ITALIAN GP

◄▲ A Hawaiian shirt on his head – the blue and white Hawaiian design is possibly Vale's most famous helmet.

ROSSI LIDS

Valentino has always been big into graphic design. No better way to illustrate that than with a decade's worth of his AGV helmets

2001 – 500 WORLD CHAMPIONSHIP

◄► Rear of 2001 lid includes a snapshot of Vale's graphic past (from left): the original number 46, Rossifumi, the sun, Valentinik, the moon and his 250-title-winning logo.

2001 – 500 WORLD CHAMPIONSHIP

◀ Valentino turned his back on the sun and the moon and headed off down psychedelia avenue with this 2001 helmet, designer Aldo Drudi adding some Aboriginal touches as he used on the helmets of Aussie former 500 champ Mick Doohan.

2002 ITALIAN GP

▼▶ This helmet paid homage to his dad's late '70s helmet design – a red, white and green lightning flash. The mini logos indicate crucial factors in the Italian psyche – sun, sea, music, motorcycles, the family, espresso coffee and so on.

2003 VALENCIA GP

▼ He returned to the flower power theme at Valencia 2003. The design was based on the winning entry of a competition arranged by sponsors Repsol.

WINTER TESTING – NOVEMBER 2004

◄▼ Mimicking a well-known brand of washing powder, this lid was a big 'up-yours' to Honda and Gibernau, who (Valentino believes) used dirty tricks to relegate him to the back of the grid at Qatar. The rear panel features washing instructions for a perfect World Championship: 125s are slightly dirty, 250s are averagely dirty, 500s are very dirty, MotoGP is extremely dirty, ultra dirty and, finally, impossibly dirty.

2004 ITALIAN GP

▲► Vale made fun of himself with this 'wooden' helmet carved from solid teak (honest) after he'd suffered two consecutive fourth-place finishes at the start of 2004. In Italian lore the fourth-place finisher gets a wooden trophy, hence the wood effect and the number four medal on the helmet's crown.

valentino
YAMAHA
GAULOISES
DAINESE
MICHELIN
46
G.P. CATALUNYA
2004

ROSSI RELIGION

It's a very special kind of Sunday worship

Sunday morning, Catalunya 2004 – just another normal moment in the life of Valentino Rossi. Out the back door of the pits and he's mobbed by fans. By the time most riders are back in their motorhomes and in the shower, Vale is still working the felt tip. Manager Gibo Badioli (grey hair, left) and minder Max (with yellow towel around his neck) are ready to pounce on anyone getting too keen.

MILAGRO

► Some girls are prepared to do anything to get their man.
HENK KEULEMANS

▲ The supporters' club make some noise up on the hill at Mugello.
GOLD AND GOOSE

► This man is a very, very big fan of Valentino Rossi. Some day his back will be worth a lot of money.
GOLD AND GOOSE

THE NURSE

► Frankly rather worrying – an Aussie fan wears his heart in his hairdo.
GOLD AND GOOSE

▼The yellow peril: Rossi fans in a high state of excitement, Le Mans 2004.
GOLD AND GOOSE

►Imitation is the sincerest form of flattery – Italian fans get into the party spirit in downtown Mugello, June 2004.
FRATERNALI

7
Bieffe

▲What a difference a couple of decades make: Graziano and Valentino at the 1980 Italian GP (where dad finished third behind King Kenny Roberts and Franco Uncini) and together again at the 2003 Italian GP.
KEULEMANS

GROWING UP FAST

Just an ordinary kid from an ordinary family. Well, not exactly…

◀Look into those eyes, look right into those eyes. Riding shotgun with dad Graziano at a Pesaro town festival in the summer of 1985, Valentino already knows exactly where he's going… The bike is the Morbidelli 500 that papa Rossi rode in the 1981 500 World Championship.
FRATERNALI

It's the summer of '85, Madonna's 'Like A Virgin' is pumping out across the town squares of Italy, annoying the Roman Catholic church, and motorcycle GP racing is an all-American affair, with 'Fast' Freddie Spencer and 'Steady' Eddie Lawson duking it out for the 500 World Championship, biking's biggest prize. Down in the Adriatic seaside town of Pesaro they're putting on a bit of a fiesta – riding racing motorcycles and cars around the centre of town, just for the sheer hell of it, because that's what they do in Italy.

Graziano Rossi has already been retired from bike racing for three years, following a massive crash at Imola, but is asked to take his old Morbidelli 500 GP bike out for a spin. Rossi lives only a few miles inland in Tavullia, and the Morbidelli factory is just down the road, so this means something to the locals. Only one little problem, Rossi's six-year-old son wants to come along for the ride.

Of course, Graziano is an accommodating sort of a guy, so he lifts Valentino onto the 500's fat aluminium fuel tank and trundles off down the road, taking it nice and easy because the kid's not even wearing a helmet, just shirt, shorts and sandals.

The fickle four-cylinder two-stroke, which Rossi raced without success in the 1981 500 World Championship, wasn't built for cruising around town, so the engine's spitting and cursing and the slick tyres are dead cold. But Valentino isn't worried in the slightest, in fact the serenity in his eyes is astonishing. He's looking ahead, working out the racing line, like he already knows exactly where he's going in life.

Except it would be wrong to say that Valentino knew exactly where he was going. Sure, he grew up surrounded by the tools of his dad's trade – engines, GP bikes, rally cars, race trucks, caravans, leathers, helmets and so on – but the only thing of which he was sure was that he wanted to go somewhere fast in life. He could just as easily have become a car racer: indeed that's what Graziano wanted, because he'd been bitten too often in nasty motorcycle crashes and didn't want his son to get so badly beaten up.

His mum, Stefania, wanted Vale to be an engineer, or a guitarist, or maybe even a footballer, anything but a racer. She had already spent too many anxious hours in hospital waiting rooms, wondering if Graziano would pull through from his all too frequent accidents.

But when Valentino was five, Graziano built him a go-kart, a wildly over-powered go-kart. 'That first kart was an awful thing,' dad remembers. 'The frame was meant for a ten-year-old, with a 60cc engine, but I put in a 100cc engine, so it was very fast and also very light, because Valentino was so little, so the thing was sliding everywhere.' And this was Valentino's initiation into speed – no wonder he's so good at controlling outrageously powerful motorcycles.

The kid was good at driving, good enough to win a regional kart title in 1990 and have his eyes set on the 1992 Italian and European championships. Then along came minimoto, the pocket-bike craze that swept through Italy in the early '90s. Valentino badly wanted his own minimoto bike: 'I push, push, push and finally Graziano buy me a minimoto. It was all-black, like Ron Haslam's Elf GP bike. It was a toy, I wanted it.' Of course, Graziano didn't have a clue what he was getting himself into… ■

‘Even his teachers at kindergarten used to say he was a leader’

Stefania Rossi

Mum and Valentino rocking the early ’80s style. ‘Valentino never gave me any problems as a kid,’ recalls Stefania. ‘At kindergarten and primary school he was the kind of boy who would get all the other kids together. He was always bright but he had more problems at secondary school because he didn’t feel like studying. He always had a great memory though, so I’d read his school books to him while he lay on the couch and he’d get what he needed from that.’ Too right, Valentino’s acute intelligence is his most important weapon on the racetrack.

ROSSI ARCHIVE

◄ The day that changed his life – Valentino is two and a bit years old and dad has just bought him his very first bike. The outrigger wheels didn't stay for long.

ROSSI ARCHIVE

◄ Dad's old racing lid, man-sized goggles – but there's no doubt about it. Right now he thinks he's the coolest kid in the whole damn universe. And he's not entirely wrong.

ROSSI ARCHIVE

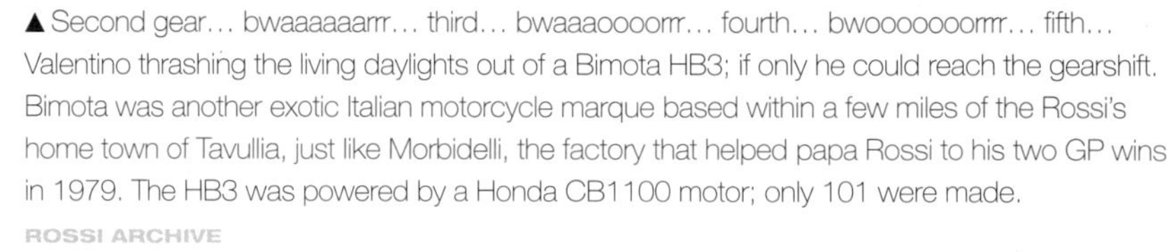

▲ Second gear… bwaaaaaarrr… third… bwaaaoooorrr… fourth… bwoooooooorrr… fifth… Valentino thrashing the living daylights out of a Bimota HB3; if only he could reach the gearshift. Bimota was another exotic Italian motorcycle marque based within a few miles of the Rossi's home town of Tavullia, just like Morbidelli, the factory that helped papa Rossi to his two GP wins in 1979. The HB3 was powered by a Honda CB1100 motor; only 101 were made.

ROSSI ARCHIVE

◀ Graziano didn't waste any time in getting Vale logo'd up. But dad's career was already on the downward slope. A big car rallying crash before the 1980 season ruined what should've been the chance of a lifetime – a factory Suzuki 500 ride.

ROSSI ARCHIVE

3

'That first kart was an awful thing… sliding everywhere!'

Graziano Rossi

Right foot stamping on the throttle, full opposite lock and a face that's all concentration and aggression – this is how Valentino learned his first lessons about throttle versus traction. From the age of five, Graziano would take little Vale down the local gravel pit, where he was almost always faster than the grown-ups in their beat-up rally cars.
ROSSI ARCHIVE

▲► 'Oh, oh, child, way you shake that thing, gonna make you burn, gonna make you sting...' Valentino may not have heard of Led Zeppelin when he was eight years old but his mum and dad sure had (take another look at Graziano's hair if you're unsure). Anyway, he quite fancied himself as a guitarist. 'Bikes were always his main interest, the only other thing he was into was guitar lessons,' mum remembers. 'He took them for six years and really liked it, even though he had a very traditional teacher.'
ROSSI ARCHIVE

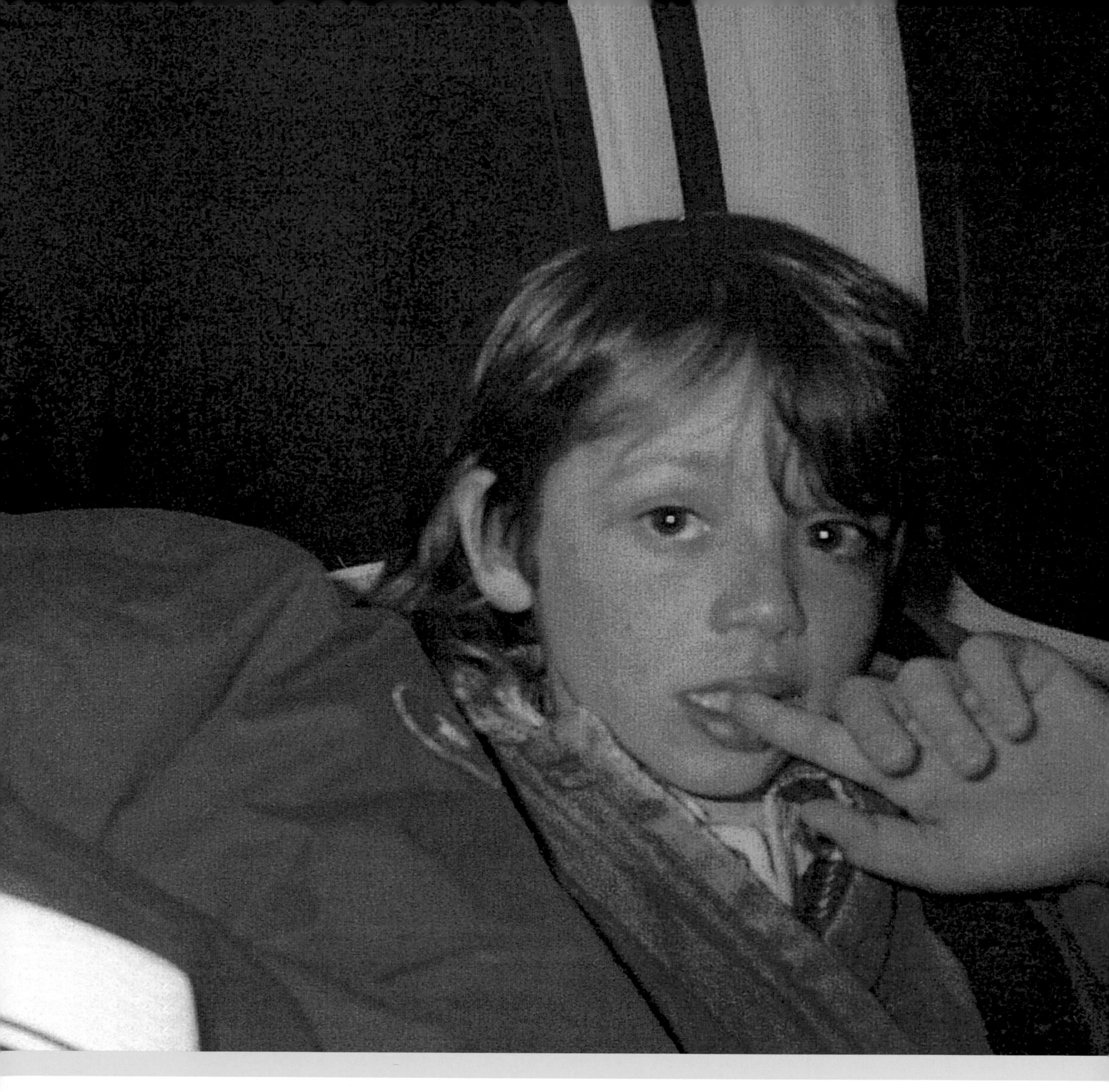

▶ They've got schoolboy racing all worked out in Italy: the kids let rip on the racetrack, the dads hit the bar. 'Hey Graziano, if Vale win again, you buy me another gin-tonic.' Ninja Turtle and Kevin Schwantz-replica helmet (Vale was a big fan of the 1993 500 World Champ) were essential items in Vale's minimoto kit. But tattered motocross shirt suggests that the Turtle wasn't always a reliable guardian angel.
ROSSI ARCHIVE

'I still remember my first minimoto win, it was funny'

At first Valentino rode his minimoto just for fun, thrashing up and down the drive outside his dad's house in Tavullia or racing mates at the dozens of Lilliputian racetracks that spread like a rash around the seaside resorts of Miramare, Cattolica and Rimini. He won his first real minimoto race in the summer of '91 and quickly realised this was heaps more fun than kart racing. And anyway, karts were getting too expensive for the Rossis.

By '92 he was local minimoto champ and brave enough to make an under-age and illegal debut on a man-sized motorcycle on a proper racetrack. 'My friend signed on, then I wore his leathers, it was like a dream.' In March '93 Valentino made his race debut at a freezing cold Maggione, aboard a Cagiva 125 streetbike: 'It was the first practice and first proper bike race of my life. I try morning practice, first corner I crash. So I come back to the pit, stay quiet, restart, make three or four laps and another crash, so we think maybe we make big mistake.'

Pretty soon he got the hang of it, however. That summer he took third in the Italian 125 streetbike series and won the crown the following year. In '95 he took the Italian 125 GP title and ventured abroad for the first time, taking third in the European 125 championship, enough to guarantee himself a ride in the '96 125 World Championship. ■

Arai
910
52

► Of course, he didn't always get it right. Getting too cocky for the camera, Vale gives his first minimoto a tad too much throttle.
ROSSI ARCHIVE

▲ You little show-off… performing a perfect one-handed wheelie in dad's driveway. It was already obvious that he had uncanny balance.
ROSSI ARCHIVE

▼ Oh what a surprise, he's a great skier too. Valentino still takes to the piste in the Italian Alps every winter but these days he's a snowboarder, not a skier.

ROSSI ARCHIVE

◀ This is the scooter-engined Ape trike he drove to high school. 'He wouldn't get the bus like everyone else,' says Stefania. 'He would wake up at the last minute, grab the Ape and fly down the hill into Pesaro.' Within weeks, all his mates had them.

FRATERNALI

▲ Just 14 years old and aboard his first man-sized bike. This is the Cagiva Mito 125 he crashed twice within a few laps during his first proper track outing at Maggione in the spring of '93.
FRATERNALI

► On the podium at Misano with Andrea Ballerini (left) and winner Roberto Locatelli, who went on to capture the 2000 125 world title.
ROSSI ARCHIVE

▼ Proud dad, or what? Vale's just finished third in the Misano round of the '93 125 Sport Production series and Graziano can't conceal his joy.
ROSSI ARCHIVE

▲ His first try-out for a top team, in late '93. Team Pileri ran Nobby Ueda and Fausto Gresini in the '93 125 world series. Ueda later became Vale's toughest 125 rival, while Gresini went on to run Sete Gibernau's MotoGP squad.

FRATERNALI

◀ Now he's really rocking. Vale poses aboard his fully painted-up Cagiva Mito at the start of the '94 Italian Sport Production championship. He won it, of course.

FRATERNALI

▼ On a real GP bike at last, Valentino raced this Sandroni-framed Aprilia to third in the '95 European championship, good enough to guarantee him a start in the following year's 125 world championship.

FRATERNALI

And so the legend begins. Having grandly outfoxed former world champ Jorge Martinez, Vale swoops towards the chequered flag to win his first GP on the afternoon of August 18 1996. Note lack of interest from pit lane.

GOLD AND GOOSE

125s

IN THE BEGINNING

Valentino Rossi was just another crash-happy teenager when he came to GPs in 1996

Oh yes, back then he had a real knack for falling off motorcycles, as well as a huge appetite for fun and an outrageous mop of girlie hair, as friend and former 125 rival Nobby Ueda remembers: 'Valentino came to stay at my house in Nagoya before the '96 Japanese GP. I introduced him to my friends as the next World Champion and they thought he was a girl! His hair was very long…'

Vale's hair stayed long throughout '96, just like he stayed a crash-happy teenager. During that season's 15 GPs he threw his little Aprilia down the road something like 18 times and he only won a single race, his debut victory at Brno during August. So Rossi was no overnight sensation – by the end of '96 no-one had any idea of the greatness that lay ahead. However, by the end of '97 he was 125 World Champion and a bona fide superstar. ▶

▶ During that second 125 season he won 11 GPs from 15 starts, all the while developing the talent that would allow him to go on to dominate every GP category – from 125s to 250s and from 500s to MotoGP. But what really grabbed everyone's attention that summer was Rossi's hilarious post-race theatrics. One weekend he would take a blow-up doll for a ride on his victory lap, the next he'd arrive on the podium dressed like superman. 'When I came to GPs all the riders were very, very serious, so when I started winning, me and my friends decided we should try to make some big fun,' Vale recalls. These comic displays made him much, much more than just another fast man on a motorcycle. They turned all kinds of people on to Valentino Rossi, ultimately transforming him into the biggest bike racing star the world has ever seen.

Of course, it was no real surprise that Vale crashed a lot when he started GP racing. Most fast racers crash a lot when they start out, because they're hurrying to find the limit and, in finding it, they invariably overstep it. 'I make some good races in '96 but also some big crazy mistakes,' Vale remembers. Most importantly, he was learning all the time and that Brno win reinforced his self-confidence, so when Aprilia equipped him with factory-prepared bikes for '97 he knew he was in with a chance of the world title. With a better bike, he crashed much less and won much more: 'I changed because when you understand your power you become more confident and with a faster engine you can be more relaxed.'

And if his growing self-confidence changed his racing, his burgeoning popularity changed his life. Ueda again: 'At the end of '97 I went to the Milan bike show and was surprised there were so many girls after Valentino. He had seven or eight security around him – big macho men – otherwise he wouldn't have been able to move. He arrived saying 'Incredible, what can I do? I want to get away,' so I helped him escape out the back.' ■

▼ Getting messy with the bubbly after beating Masaki Tokudome at the '97 British GP. He won so many races that summer that he wrapped up the championship with three races to go.
GOLD AND GOOSE

▲Hanging in his bedroom, summer of '97. Check the rude graffiti on the Biaggi poster. Apart from casting aspersions on the Roman's sexuality, the scribble also suggests that the reigning 250 champ 'doesn't even deserve a Benelli triple', that 'Biaggi is nothing' and that 'Biaggi = Naples' (another Italian insult).

FRATERNALI

◀Just another long-haired kid showing off down the local shopping mall. Or something like that.

FRATERNALI

▼Valentino shows off his first 'hospitality unit' in the Imola paddock, July 1997. Compare this to dad's hospitality 'bus' at Imola '81 (see page 129).

FRATERNALI

ROSSIFUMI
Comel
FUCK
21
46
Nastro Azzurro
polini
aprilia
DUNLOP
GAS

'I make some good races but also some big crazy mistakes'

◀ Life is never less than hectic in 125 racing – this is Vale trying to make good his escape at Brno '97, chased by Scalvini, Ueda, Manako, Martinez, Sakata and the rest. Twenty minutes later he was world champ.

GOLD AND GOOSE

▲ Following a big bang to his head (when dad crashed a car after Vale's title-winning party in Tavullia) Valentino entered his infamous surrealist period. Don't even ask…

VITALE

▼ Looking after number one: celebrating his very first world title atop the Brno podium, 31 August 1997.
VITALE

► 'Ciao, mama! I am the champion!' Vale phones home from the Brno pits. From now the Italian media would be bugging him non-stop. It took him a while to realise they weren't all his mates.
VITALE

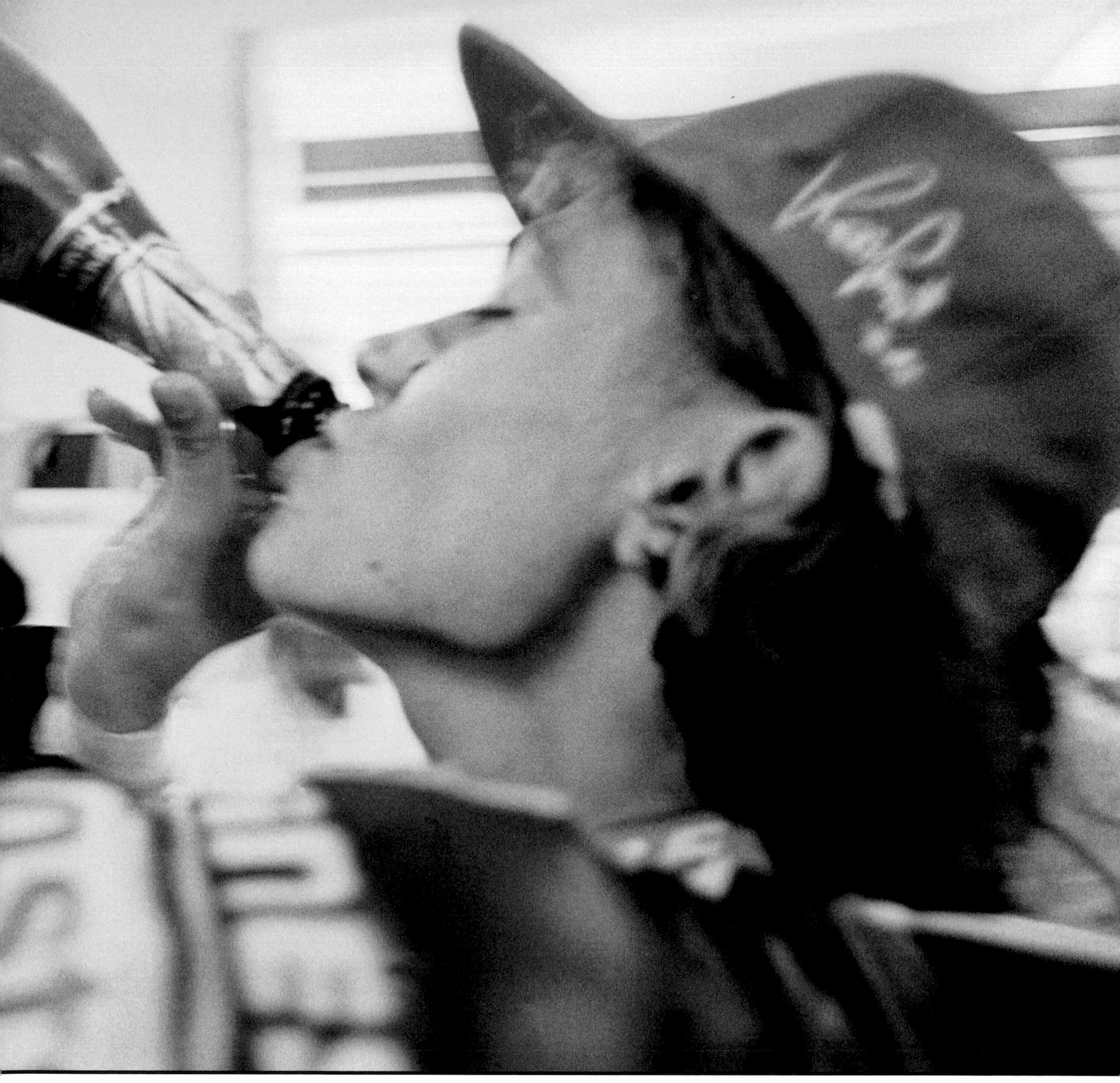

'Becoming world champion is for sure the greatest moment and maybe the first was best'

▲ The first taste is the sweetest. Getting stuck into the fizz after wrapping up the 125 world title. He still rates this moment as sweet as winning the 500 and MotoGP crowns.
VITALE

OSSIFUMI
ICIAL FANS CLUB

◀ Within minutes of winning the title, he was back in his tiny camper van with his mates, drinkin', smokin' and generally behaving like a grown-up.

VITALE

▼ Falling prey to a minor attack of pre-race nerves. Of course, there was no need to worry.

VITALE

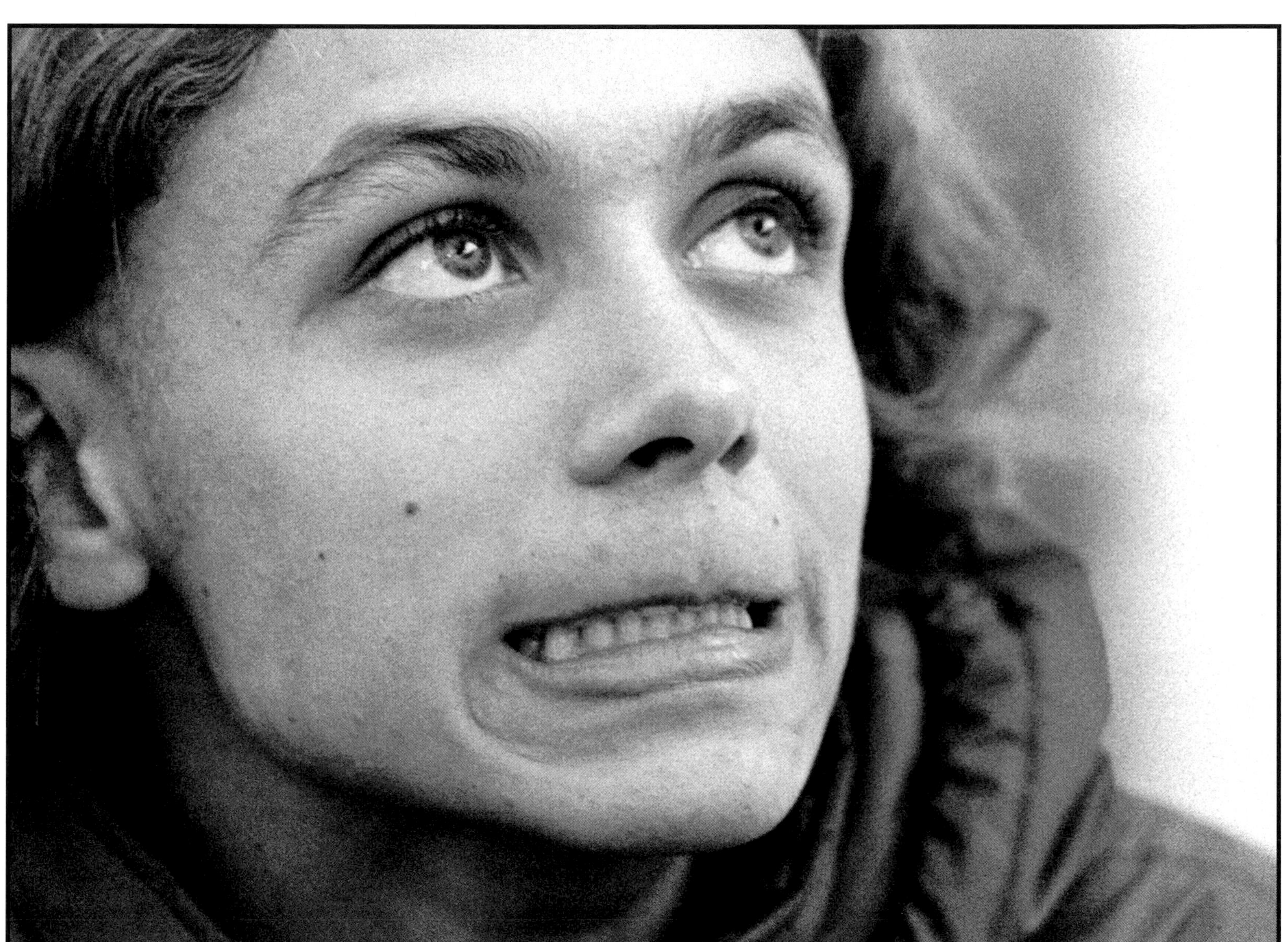

Valentino had to work hard for that first title. Although he'd already won nine of the season's first 11 races, he wasn't able seal the championship with a win at Brno, where he'd won his first GP success 12 months earlier. Still aching from a crash during Saturday's final qualifying session and unhappy with the set-up of his Aprilia, he spent the entire 19 laps in the midst of an insane dogfight with nine rivals. He eventually finished the race in third spot, just 0.328 seconds behind winner Nobby Ueda, and just enough to give him the title. Of course, the fun was only just beginning. On his slowdown lap Vale stopped to pick up a massive number one – carved out of solid granite (or possibly Styrofoam) – that his fan club strapped to his back. 'Vord Cienpion' proclaimed the prop, and it wasn't wrong. Minutes later he stood on the podium with his dad while the sombre tones of the Japanese national anthem rang out. After that, chaos! With half a bottle of champagne inside him, Vale headed home to his camper van in the paddock and proceeded to get very merry with his mates. A few weeks later his home town laid on a massive celebration, Tavullia's main square packed with a thousand fans who partied into the night. It was the first of many Tavullia parties… ■

▲ Listen up! Addressing the crowd at the start of his Tavullia title-celebration party, a few weeks after he had secured the crown at Brno.
VITALE

▲ Vale's first fans – no smoke without fire.
VITALE

▼ Uccio and Vale slightly the worse for wear in the dying stages of the Tavullia knees-up.
VITALE

► Too much beer.
VITALE

46
BREIL
DIESEL
RADIO
DEEJAY

Vale's gangly limbs fitted a 250 better than a 125. And it didn't take him long to master the fast but fickle Aprilia RSW250.
GOLD AND GOOSE

250s

THE WORLD ON HIS SHOULDERS

He may have been bound for greatness, but life got tough when Valentino moved from 125s to 250s

The toughest time of his life – that's how Valentino describes his two seasons in the 250 World Championship. Not that the racing was the hardest (he won 14 of his 30 races in the class) but this was when he began to learn the heavy price of fame, when his beaming teenage naivety was rudely snuffed out by the big, bad world. Not only that, two of his best mates died in a car crash.

When he first climbed on to a 250 at the end of '97, Valentino was still a wide-eyed 18-year-old, loving all the attention from the media and his fans, loving everything about life, about racing. He hadn't quite realised that he had unwittingly signed a Faustian pact – make the people and the press love you and you're ▶

► From boy to man. He was a sweet-faced 19-year-old kid when he fronted up for pre-season testing in '98. The next few months would have a huge effect on his character, hardening him for the challenges ahead.
GOLD AND GOOSE

► in for a rollercoaster of a love affair. Even when everything was sweet, sometimes there was just too much love: 'Now everyone in Italy recognises me,' he said. 'It's "Rossi! Rossi! Rossi!" all the time, I don't like!' No wonder that by the time he'd won the 250 title in October '99 he was already making plans to escape his homeland for the anonymity of London.

So '98 and '99 were all about coming of age, about leaving his carefree teenage years behind. And about learning to ride bigger bikes, of course: 250s were an important staging post on his journey to MotoGP greatness, not that there was any certainty that he'd even make it that far. All Valentino had done so far was win a single 125 world title: there had been no conclusive evidence that this kid might be the most gifted bike racer to have walked this planet.

From the get-go he was fast on 250s, but also flawed. He crashed out of four of the first ten races of '98, then bounced back to win the final four, only missing the title by three points. In theory, the '99 championship should've been a walkover but a few bike problems in the early races plus a miserable ride in the soaking-wet Japanese GP ('I don't like to ride under the water') gave him a mountain to climb. After that Vale got his head down to win eight of the last 12 races, finally alerting the world to the fact that he might be a bit special after all.

'Very much was expected of me when I came to 250s in 1998, so it was the most difficult period of my career, I really felt the pressure,' explains Vale, who had full-factory Aprilias for both his seasons in the class. 'I was fast but I made mistakes because I wasn't calm, because I had some personal problems with some friends who I realised weren't friends. It took some time to understand that.'

The best thing about his two years in 250s was getting up late: 'In 125s I had to get up for morning practice at seven, for 500s at eight, but in 250s I could stay in bed till nine!' No wonder he overslept for 500 morning practice at Catalunya in 2000. ■

▲ Not quite ready to put away childish things, Valentino kills some time in the Mugello pits during winter testing prior to his first 250 season. Pretty soon he'd be able to afford much, much more than just a pink toy Cadillac.
MILAGRO

► Throwing himself to the mercy of 100,000 Dutch mullets as he celebrates his very first 250 win at the '98 Assen TT. This win followed a rash of morale-sapping crashes but even then Vale wasn't out of the wilderness. It wasn't until later in '98 that he assumed mastery of the class.
KEULEMANS

Nastro
Azzurro
aprilia
BREIL
domino
DUNLOP
DAINESE
ROSSIFUMI
aprilia

► The '70s theme was something he'd return to later, at Valencia 2003.
GOLD AND GOOSE

Mugello '99 was Valentino's Day: one big Rossi Love-In. It ended with Vale prostrate on the tarmac, with a couple of hundred over-excited fans on top of him. He hadn't planned it like this, though you could say he'd asked for it, racing an Aprilia sprayed up in eye-watering yellow and turquoise swirls, emblazoned with the '70s-inspired legend ValentiPeace&Love. The race itself had been relatively easy – a comfortable three-second win over German veteran Ralf Waldmann – but the victory lap turned out to be an altogether tougher proposition. Things went okay until he reached Casanova Savelli, the heart-stopping downhill right/left where his fan club camps out in its thousands (because this is where Rossi watched his first GP in 1991). A few yards further round the track he ran into Italian cameraman Gigi Soldano (the man responsible for many of the Milagro images in this book) and crashed to the ground. In an instant he was submerged in the throng, gasping for breath as 1000 Rossi worshippers did anything to get a piece of him – gloves, helmet, arms, legs. So was this the day he finally decided to escape the homeland hubbub and move to London? ■

'The fans went crazy, I think I would die'

▲ In a vain effort to avoid a cameraman, Valentino loses it despite the best efforts of a couple of panicking fans... topples to the tarmac, Italian tricolore still in hand... and gets swamped by a mass of writhing, sweaty bodies.

GOLD AND GOOSE/FRATERNALI

▲ By now there was no way he could head out for a gentle evening cruise around the paddock. Whatever colour he dyed his hair, people were on to him, although going red, white and green at Imola was hardly keeping it incognito.
GOLD AND GOOSE

► Getting artful with his lines, Valentino leads Shinya Nakano (Yamaha) and Tohru Ukawa (Honda), two of his biggest rivals for the 1999 250 world title. This Jerez win was his first of '99, after a couple of disasters at the season-opening Malaysian and Japanese GPs that left him a gaping 21 points down on the championship leaders.
GOLD AND GOOSE

46
BREIL
PlayStation
Nastro Azzurro
aprilia
TIM
DUNLOP

▲ His Aprilia proudly painted in the red, white and green of the Italian tricolore, Vale wastes Stefano Perugini (4), Olivier Jacque (19) and the rest at the Imola '98 GP. This success was the first of four straight victories that brought him to within just three points of winning the 250 world title at his first attempt. If only he hadn't crashed out of four races that summer.

GOLD AND GOOSE

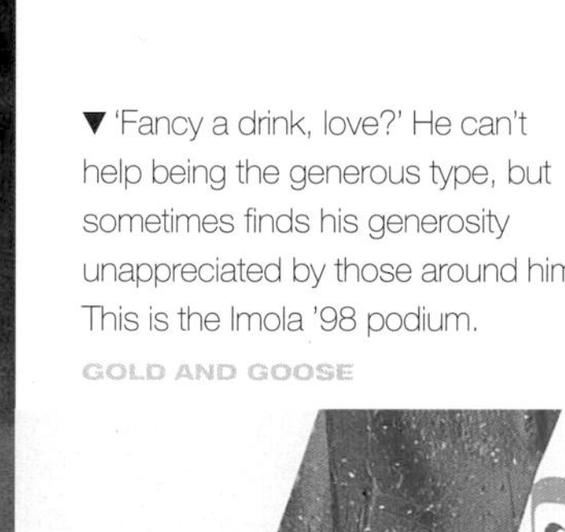

▼ 'Fancy a drink, love?' He can't help being the generous type, but sometimes finds his generosity unappreciated by those around him. This is the Imola '98 podium.

GOLD AND GOOSE

◀ Rossi and team-mate Tetsuya Harada get introduced to the locals before the '98 Japanese GP. The large gents were students from a Tokyo sumo college but declined an invitation to become 'brolly dollies' for Sunday's races. Big blokes but shy, you see.

KEULEMANS

46
HONDA
BREIL
Nastro
65
Emerson
elf

Mugello 2000: Vale stuffs it up the inside of Kenny Roberts Junior (2). Loris Capirossi (65), Norick Abe, Nobu Aoki (both behind Roberts), Carlos Checa (7) and Max Biaggi (4) give chase. Capirossi won after Valentino and Biaggi fell.

BARSHON

500s

PREMIER LEAGUE CHAMP

It took just two years for Valentino to conquer the 500s

In the real world, winning a 125 or 250 world title means not a lot, a bit like winning a second or third division football title. It's merely another step on the journey towards the main prize – the premier league.

When Valentino joined bike racing's premier division in 2000 there were just two years left in which he could win the 500 title, the class that had been the Big Deal ever since the birth of World Championship bike racing way back in 1949. The sport's governing body had decided that from 2002 the scary old two-stroke 500s would be replaced by a new breed of more sophisticated 990cc four-strokes, more relevant to the machines sold on the street. Vale had spent half his childhood dreaming about winning the 500 crown, now he had just two seasons in which ▶

▼ The men who made him king. From left: Rossano Brazzi, who guided Vale to the 1999 250 title; Mauro Noccioli, who helped him to the 1997 125 crown; and Jeremy Burgess, who masterminded his successful assault on the 500 World Championship in 2001.
MILAGRO

▶ to master the scariest motorcycles known to man…

And there was no certainty that he'd ever make it as a great 500 rider. If someone had told you in April 2000 that Valentino wasn't half as good as he was cracked up to be, you would have struggled to disagree with them. The 21-year-old hadn't made the greatest of starts to his 500 career, and in fact his entry into the premier league had been an unmitigated disaster. His first three races produced two crashes and one 11th-place finish. Valentino, some people opined, could handle a puny 125 or 250 but he couldn't ride a real man's motorcycle.

Of course, the signs of greatness were there for anyone bothered to look carefully enough. He had battled for a front-row start at his very first 500 GP and set the fastest lap of the race before his 190 horsepower Honda NSR500 rudely ejected him on to the tarmac. And, anyway, it didn't take too long to prove that he really could ride a man's bike: first podium in his third outing, first win after just eight races, in tricky, damp conditions at Donington Park.

By the end of the following season no-one was in any doubt. Valentino had won two 500 GPs during 2000 to end the year second overall and he grew to dominate in 2001, winning 11 out of 16 races. In just two seasons he had eclipsed the victory rate of Mick Doohan, the rock-hard Aussie who dominated premier-league racing in the '90s with 54 GP victories and five back-to-back titles.

Vale had also taken on and defeated his first serious rival, Max Biaggi. While most of his 125 and 250 opponents had also been mates, he enjoyed a relationship of mutual hatred with the Roman Emperor. Their rivalry threatened to spiral out of control after their notorious punch-up in June 2001, but Valentino stayed cool to soundly defeat his compatriot.

And while Vale's more recent MotoGP achievements seem to overshadow his 500 successes, he still believes that the 500 is the apogee of racing motorcycles, an altogether nastier beast than a cuddly four-stroke MotoGP bike. 'The 500's power was more wild, so the bike was more difficult to ride,' he says. 'But if you took risks, you could make the difference against the others.' ■

▶ The winning secret: a plate of pasta and a bottle of ice-cold Nastro. This is Welkom, South Africa, 2001, one of those flyaway races where the MotoGP paddock roughs it in Portakabins, rather than the five-star transporters and motorhomes they inhabit at European races.
MILAGRO

▶▶ Valentino became an ex-pat in 2000, moving to London to escape the attentions of his omnipresent Italian fans. He rented a flat in St James Square, London, then bought a place in Mayfair. Getting about the posh part of town was easy – aboard a blagged Honda SP-2.
GOLD AND GOOSE

PlayStation
polini
Nastro Azzurro
HONDA
46
BREIL
polini
Nastro Azzurro
HRC
VTR

GOLD & GOOSE

'Is necessary to have big balls to ride the 500'

► Vale and Biaggi get stuck into each other at the 2000 Portuguese GP, but this time they're only fighting over third place. Vale was still learning the art of 500 riding at this stage, even though he'd just won his first big-bike race at a damp Donington Park a few weeks earlier.
BARSHON

BREIL
46
HONDA
agv

▶ Decisions, decisions… Vale deep in thought during 2001 Italian GP qualifying with JB and Showa suspension technician Juan Martinez (now Gibernau's crew chief). The blur is Uccio.

GOLD AND GOOSE

▼ The best laid plans of mice and men… Even this three-way pre-race snog didn't help Vale at Mugello. He crashed on the sighting lap, then again in the rain-lashed race.

MILAGRO

▲ Vale's bright idea of going Hawaiian for Mugello 2001 didn't just mean making his bike, leathers and team gear blue and white. This is Uccio's dad and the fan club making merry in the paddock.

MILAGRO

▶ Hawaii Five-0-0. Vale took the beach party to the racetrack at Mugello, but while the Hawaii paint job looked great in sunny practice, it didn't look so good upside down in the mud on race day.

GOLD AND GOOSE

agv
46
IL DOTTORE
'EN<RGIE
BREIL
MANPOWER
domino
HONDA
PlayStation 2
polini
Birra · Beer
Nastro Azzurro
Export Lager
MICHELIN
brembo
NGK
RK
TAKASAGO CHAIN
AFAM
FOX
MARIANI KALOR
BIO
SHOWA

▲ Mine, all mine! Valentino hugs the trophy after blitzing Biaggi in the 2001 British GP. A big crash during practice had left him way down the grid but he still managed to win. Even now he rates this victory his most thrilling.

GOLD AND GOOSE

► All the better for seeing you with… Vale gives himself a patent Rossi eye massage on the grid for the 2000 Portuguese GP. It's all about increasing blood flow, apparently.

GOLD AND GOOSE

'I think Brno is the masterpiece of my career'

▲ Brno 2001: The moment that effectively decided the outcome of the final 500 World Championship. Vale shadowed Biaggi until the Roman overcooked it and crashed. From this moment on, he had the upper hand over his bitter rival.

GOLD AND GOOSE

► The secret price of winning the 500 title. Former 500 GP clown Randy Mamola cream pies Vale during the post-race press conference at Phillip Island, where he'd secured the title with a breathtaking win, a fraction ahead of Biaggi and Capirossi.

BARSHON

▲ Things are starting to get messy at Honda's 2001 end-of-season party in Rio. Vale has made it his mission for the night to get 250 world champ Daijiro Kato well and truly hammered; 18 months later Kato was dead, suffering fatal injuries in a high-speed accident during the 2003 Japanese MotoGP race.

GOLD AND GOOSE

◀ Valentino on stage at the 2001 FIM awards, where he collected his 500 title award from FIM president Mr Burns (sorry, Francesco Zerbi). Championship runners-up Biaggi and Capirossi wear suits while Vale keeps it rebellious in jeans, trainers and no tie.

MILAGRO

▲ Randy Mamola, how do you say this… making like a lady during the Rio party. MotoGP's great and good are suitably amused. From left, Honda PR Carlo Florenzano (Hawaiian shirt), Toni Elias (bottom left, light blue shirt, then a 125 man, now Vale's fellow Yamaha MotoGP rider), Vale, 2000 250 champ Olivier Jacque (two-tone blue sweatshirt), 2002 250 champ Marco Melandri (bottom right, black top) and Dorna big cheese Carmelo Espeleta (far right, jacket).

GOLD AND GOOSE

HONDA
MICHELIN
NGK
GAS

Valentino makes some art at Valencia 2003, his last race for Honda. He won 20 of his 32 races on the factory's 210mph RCV V5.

BARSHON

MotoGP Honda

LIVING THE EASY LIFE

Valentino burned even brighter in MotoGP but winning with Honda got too easy

GP racing got turned upside down in 2002. The knife-edge 500cc two-strokes that had ruled the premier class for three decades were consigned to the dustbin of racing history, replaced by rip-snorting 990cc four-strokes. Everything changed – the bikes were much faster, much pricier and the two-strokes' spine-chilling yowl was drowned out by the four-strokes' ear-splitting boom. But the song remained the song – Valentino Rossi was still king of the racetrack.

Five months after he'd won the last-ever 500 GP at Rio in November 2001, Vale won the first-ever MotoGP event at Suzuka in April 2002. By the end of his two seasons on the RC211V V5 he'd won another 20 GP victories to take him into motorcycling's hall of fame. Only racing ▶

► Valentino and Honda's brand-new RCV distract Spanish builders, working on the new Jerez pits complex, during their first European outing in November 2001. Vale's input played a large part in the V5's amazing performance.

MILAGRO

◀ Valentino and his Repsol Honda henchmen ambush passers-by with buckets of water in the Brno paddock, August 2003. It's all part of an Italian summer water ritual, apparently.
BARSHON

▶ legends Mick Doohan, Mike Hailwood and Giacomo Agostini were still ahead of him.

But Vale's two seasons on the stunningly effective RCV were very different. He ruled 2002 with awesome precision – winning 11 of the 16 races, including a mid-season run of seven back-to-back victories, and never finishing lower than second. He won the title with four races still to go, despite recording a DNF at the Czech GP, where he suffered tyre problems. It was an impressive record for a rider on a brand-new bike in a brand-new World Championship.

If anything, 2002 had been too easy, because during 2003 Valentino seemed to run out of juice. He won just two of the season's first nine races, beaten on three occasions by new rival Sete Gibernau, now on a Honda instead of Suzuki's dog-slow GSV-R. But after the Italian media had savaged him, suggesting he was a spent force, Vale got a grip on himself to win all but one of the last seven races. The first of those six victories came at Brno, where he beat Gibernau with a daring end-of-race attack: 'After making stupid mistakes at the last two races – just from thinking too much – I changed my tactics – ride 100 per cent and if anyone comes past, attack them immediately!'

He maintained that aggressive attitude for the remainder of the season, falling out with Honda after months of very public wrangling over a new contract. So he finally decided to walk away from MotoGP's most powerful factory to ride for the struggling Yamaha outfit. 'Maybe my choice seems a little bit crazy,' said Vale. 'But we will see next year.'

Of course, those who know Valentino weren't surprised by this apparently suicidal career move: he simply wanted another challenge because he loves a challenge. As Carlo Pernat, the former Aprilia team boss who gave him his first GP ride in 1996, says: 'Two qualities make Valentino special. First, his sense of balance on the motorcycle is unbelievable, I've never seen anything like it. Second, he has fun, he amuses himself by racing. That's all he does, he amuses himself.' Which must be just a little depressing for his rivals… ■

◀ Racing for Honda took Valentino too deep into his comfort zone – after easily destroying his rivals in the first MotoGP series in 2002, he got bored.
BARSHON

'When Valentino shuts his visor and starts a race, everybody becomes his worst enemy'

Graziano Rossi

Slowly, slowly, catchy monkey. Valentino on his way to victory at Jerez 2003. He's already passed Loris Capirossi – only Nicky Hayden, Max Biaggi and Sete Gibernau to go.
BARSHON

REPSOL
HONDA
REPSOL

Incarcerated by the Italian media for a run of so-so results during 2003, Vale became prisoner 1111-46 at the Czech GP, where his RCV carried these Interpol mugshots. 'They said I was in crisis because I'd been beaten at the last four races,' he laughed after winning the Brno race to break free from jail. 'Leading the championship and finishing on the podium obviously isn't enough for them, so now I must work on the chain gang!'

The Italian media never give anyone an easy ride – they build people up to knock them down – and Rossi has long complained about the posse of Italian journos who follow him everywhere, waiting to attack whenever he makes the smallest of mistakes. As Italian opera legend Pavarotti is fond of saying: 'When a journalist write about the positive, he write five lines, when he write about the negative he become a poet.'

BARSHON

180
170
165
1111-46
OCTOR
38

▼ Groovy, baby! Vale wigs out after his final win for Honda. At this stage the world's biggest bike brand had no idea how much it was going to miss him.

BARSHON

► Receiving his leaving card from Repsol Honda boss Carlo Fiorani. Many insiders reckoned he was insane for leaving Honda but does he look the slightest bit worried?

BARSHON

▲ Hard on the gas and all crossed up, Vale shows Honda rival Sete Gibernau how it's done at Valencia.
BARSHON

46
GAULOISES
YAMAHA
DAINESE
THE DOCTOR

Standing on his M1's seat, Vale conducts the pit-lane worshippers after his stunning 2004 Malaysian GP victory. This was possibly the first 'angry' win of his career. He had scores to settle after he'd been relegated to the back row of the grid at the previous weekend's Qatar GP – and he settled them well.

MILAGRO

MotoGP Yamaha —

BECOMING GOD

When Valentino quit Honda he took the risk of his career. He would either end up a fool or a deity…

In fact Valentino wasn't becoming God at all, even if it rather seemed like it. Asked in an interview why he'd stopped celebrating his wins in madcap style, he answered 'I am becoming old', but his Italian accent obscured his words and the headlines rattled out across the world: 'Rossi: I am becoming God!'.

Of course, Vale's against-all-odds success on Yamaha's M1 did make him something more than mere genius. There are riders of a certain ability, like Max Biaggi, Sete Gibernau, Alex Criville and Kenny Roberts Junior, and there are riders of a certain nobility, like Giacomo Agostini, Mike Hailwood, King Kenny Roberts, Mick Doohan and Rossi. After his stunning 2004 World Championship success Valentino was in the pantheon, no doubt about it. ▶

▼ Like a schoolboy motocrosser with his first trophy, Valentino beams with delight after his debut win on the Yamaha at the 2004 South African GP. He scored this historic victory after a race-long duel with Max Biaggi, whose Honda was way faster.

BARSHON

► And yet it could all have gone so wrong. Yamaha wasn't in great shape when Rossi signed with Honda's old rival in autumn 2003. And Honda was bound to up the ante to ensure that the world's most powerful bike manufacturer wasn't embarrassed by this turbulent young upstart. At first, the RCV was way faster than the M1, but somehow Valentino managed to demolish the Honda hordes at the 2004 season-opening South African GP to start his Yamaha years the same way he'd finished his days at Honda. And that Welkom win made history – in more than half a century of bike GPs no-one had ever won back-to-back premier-class races on different makes of bike.

Valentino continued to defy the odds throughout 2004. Down on speed, he had to dig deeper than ever before, which is why he tumbled twice during the first few months of the season, as often as he'd crashed during his previous two years with Honda. Crew chief Jeremy Burgess had some straightforward advice at faster tracks like Mugello: 'Valentino, you're on the straight for a long time here, so keep your shoulders tucked in and your toes up'. JB's wise words worked because Vale won at Mugello and at other fast tracks. Even at the end of the year he was working harder than anyone – at Valencia he was only 14th fastest through the speed trap and yet he still won.

For 2005 it was a very different story. Informed by Vale's and JB's input, Yamaha built a much-improved M1. Honda bosses had to suffer in silence as Valentino rubbed more salt into their self-inflicted wounds. He ran away with the first half of the season, winning six of the first seven races, while his Honda rivals fell over themselves in pursuit. ■

► Giving his vital first impressions of the M1 to JB, Yamaha MotoGP chief Masahiko Nakajima (background) and engineer Ken Suzuki (who died from a brain tumour in April 2005 – RIP). 'The bike is a tool, so we have to work to get the best out of the tool,' says Valentino. 'If we have a problem with the front end, we modify the front end – it's like mathematics!'

GOLD AND GOOSE

◀ The start of a brave new adventure – striding out into the Sepang pit lane for a photo call before his first ride on the M1, January 2004. At this moment nobody knew whether his shock decision to quit Honda would prove him to be a racing genius or a petulant fool.

GOLD AND GOOSE

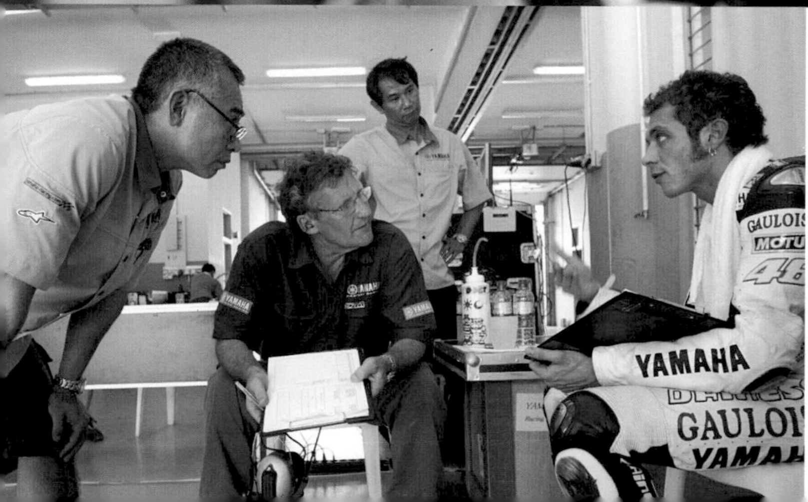

▲ From here on in, it was no longer just an impossible dream. The pit-lane TV monitors tell the Gauloises Yamaha team that they've got pole position at the season-opening Welkom GP. Team boss Davide Brivio (with Vale's Michelin technician Pierre Alves on the left) offers his congratulations. 'This first pole for Yamaha is like ten for Honda,' said Valentino.

MILAGRO

▲ Come and have a go if you think you're hard enough… Valentino taunts his new worst enemy, Gibernau, during practice for the 2004 Malaysian GP. For several years the pair had been good mates, getting drunk together after races, that sort of thing, but the events of the 2004 Qatar GP changed all that.

MILAGRO

► With just a few days to go before the next race in Malaysia, Vale casts a worried glance at his bloodied little finger after crashing out of the Qatar GP. He'd been forced to start from the back row of the grid after his crew had been caught cleaning his grid slot on the sand-blown track. Valentino reckons title rival Gibernau was a prime mover in the protest that had him punished.

MILAGRO

'Sete is behind all this, he's behaved like a child'

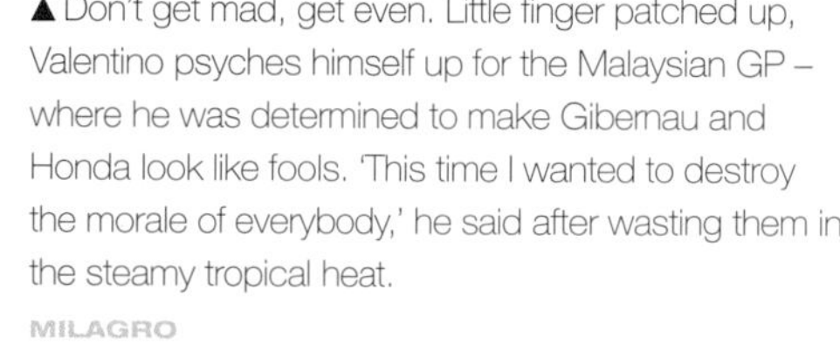

▲ Don't get mad, get even. Little finger patched up, Valentino psyches himself up for the Malaysian GP – where he was determined to make Gibernau and Honda look like fools. 'This time I wanted to destroy the morale of everybody,' he said after wasting them in the steamy tropical heat.

MILAGRO

Ecstasy in a bottle. Valentino celebrates winning the 2004 MotoGP crown at Phillip Island. All he had to do to secure the title was finish second to Gibernau – but he beat the Spaniard in a ferocious duel, despite running off the track at 120mph. His title-winning T-shirt proclaims: 'What a show!'

GOLD AND GOOSE

MICHELIN
CHE
YAMAHA
FREIXENET

▲ No need to ask who won and who lost. Valentino, cocky as hell after destroying Gibernau at the final turn of the final lap of the 2005 Spanish GP, stands atop the podium, while Gibernau looks ready for a good blub. More payback for Qatar 2004.

GOLD AND GOOSE

► Final corner, Jerez 2005: Valentino sees a gap inside Gibernau and doesn't need a written invitation. Gibernau, determined to win his home GP, shuts the door but it's already too late. The pair collide, propelling the Spaniard into the gravel trap. Gibernau extricated himself to finish second.

GOLD AND GOOSE/MILAGRO

▼ Valentino's bulldog Guido may not live with him in London (he stays with mum in Italy) but he's always along for the ride, emblazoned on the seat of his master's M1. Note Vale's respect for racing history – Guido wears old-school Yamaha colours, made famous by King Kenny Roberts in the '70s.
GOLD AND GOOSE

► Like most MotoGP riders, Vale has a massage in Dr Costa's Clinica Mobile before every ride; keeps the body loose in case of accidents.
MILAGRO

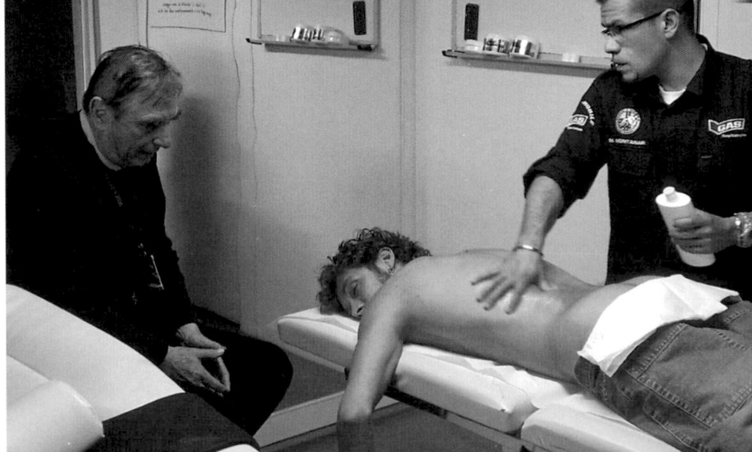

◀ Definitely a man who's always had his own way of doing things. While Gibernau (15) and Biaggi (3) peel off to complete the warm-up lap prior to the 2005 Spanish GP, Vale is busy making himself comfortable. Cool or what?

YAMAHA

▲ He spent his teenage years terrorising the Tavullia cops on a scooter, so at least he still gets to utilise those skills as an adult. And here he is on a Yamaha scooter, getting to know Shanghai's new GP circuit before the first Chinese GP in May 2005.

GOLD AND GOOSE

agv
agv
Drudi Performance
KERAKOLL
KERAKOLL

Nailing the apex on his way to pole position, Jerez 2004.

BARSHON

▲ Vale's got his head down and his front wheel up as he leads the 2004 season-ending Valencia GP from Honda rivals Makoto Tamada and Nicky Hayden. He won the race even though his M1 was only 14th quickest through the speed trap.
GOLD AND GOOSE

► The old boss meets the new boss? Fellow Italian Marco Melandri looks the man most likely to inherit Vale's mantle when the world champ retires. These two first raced together in the early '90s, on minimotos.
MILAGRO

▼Valentino and JB have built an amazing rapport in their six seasons together. In some ways they seem like father and son, although JB has only had to tell off the youngster on a few occasions, like the time Vale overslept and missed morning practice…

GOLD AND GOOSE

'A happy team is a good team. We don't take ourselves too seriously, we have a laugh'

Jeremy Burgess

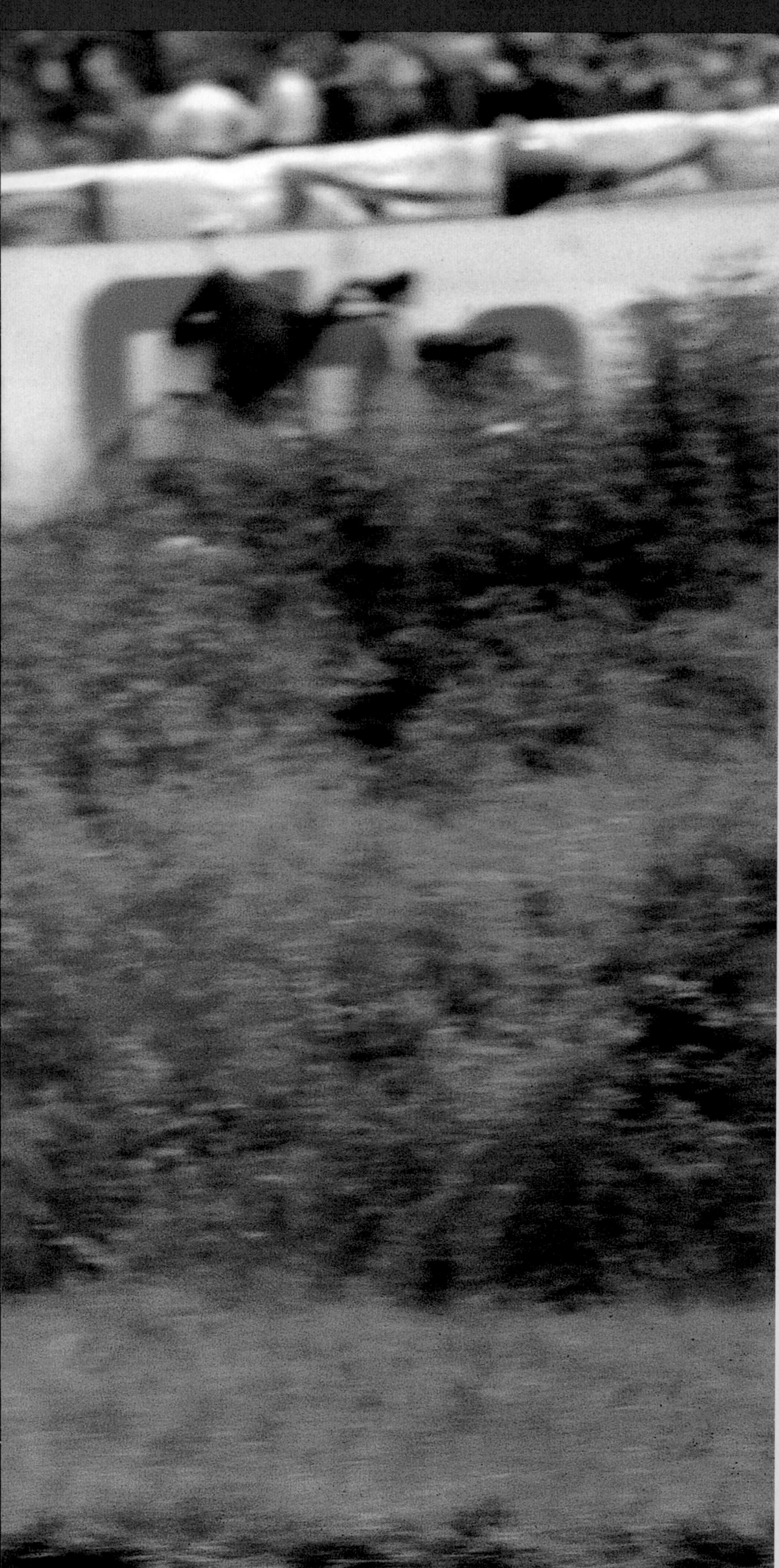

Papa Rossi on his way to victory, Dutch TT, Assen 1979.

KEULEMANS

PAPA ROSSI

To know Valentino, you need to know his dad…

Graziano's Assen victory was the second of his three 250 wins in 1979. 'Assen was my favourite because Assen is the true theatre of bikes,' he recalls. 'I start in third place, pass Kork Ballington's Kawasaki after half a lap, then some laps later I arrive behind Greg Hansford's Kawasaki. We are going down the straight side by side, we both decide to brake at the last metre, but I brake even later. Was fantastic! I make my first win at Rijeka, one week before. I qualified between the Kawasakis, who won everything in those days, so when I arrive on the grid between them they look at me like I am a UFO. That was the beautiful thing, it was a surprise, and surprises are always important in life. Maybe I lose the chance of the World Championship at Silverstone, two races later. I crash on the last lap when I come across a slow rider halfway through a fast right. I decide to pass him on the outside but this was a bad decision, very bad...' ■

▼ He could ride four-strokes too – Graziano at speed on a Bimota Honda, Imola, 1981.
FRATERNALI

▲ And just like Vale, dad loves anything with an engine and wheels. Here he entertains the crowd with some sideways antics in his clapped-out Opel rally car at the Pesaro town fiesta, summer 1985.
FRATERNALI

► The definition of Latin cool? Even with his leather dungarees, Graziano manages to cut a dash in the Misano pits with mate and 1981 500 world champ Marco Lucchinelli, summer of '84.
FRATERNALI

▼ This little Fiat was Graziano's 'hospitality unit' at the 1981 Imola GP. Rossi senior was definitely an eccentric motorcycle racer.

FRATERNALI

▲ Graziano was a bit wacky, just like his son, wacky enough to wear this hallucinatory fantasy helmet. The paint was done by artist friend Aldo Drudi, who also does Vale's graphics.

OXLEY

HONDA NSR500

2001

METAL ROSSI

The bikes that have transported Valentino to premier-class World Championship success

Valentino has ruled the premier class pretty much since he first turned up at the start of the 2000 season. He didn't quite win the title that year but he has won it every year since and has achieved that remarkable run of success on three very different motorcycles. First, the harum-scarum Honda NSR, the last of the man-eating two-stroke 500s; then Honda's wondrous RCV four-stroke, possibly the most intelligently created race bike in history; and finally the Yamaha YZR-M1, the machine that Vale turned from loser to winner in a few short months. Motorcycles don't get any more trick than these three: they're all fabulous works of art, a testament to the greatest engineers on this planet.

Massive carbon-fibre airbox delivers air to the NSR's greedy Keihin carbs, no hi-tech fuel injection on this 'stinkwheel'. Monster aluminium chassis just about keeps the motor under control.

STUDIO PHOTOS:
TERUTAKA HOASHI/RIDERS CLUB

HONDA NSR500 2001

This is the Honda NSR500 two-stroke that took Valentino to his first premier-class title in 2001. It's a history-making machine, because that year's 500 World Championship was the last before new technical regulations admitted the 990cc four-strokes that dominate the sport today. It's also an evil machine – fickle, fiery and ferocious compared to the more rider-friendly four-strokes. Nevertheless the 2001 NSR was the apogee of high-performance two-stroke engineering, a science now restricted to the 250 and 125 GP classes.

Honda built its first NSR500 in 1984, so almost two decades of development went into the bike that Valentino rode. Throughout its time on the tracks the NSR was always a tower of power, rocketing American legend Freddie Spencer around the Daytona banking at 190mph on its 1984 race debut. By 2001 the NSR V4 was pumping out almost 200 horsepower but with superb throttle linearity. It was this remarkable usability that made it the bike that every GP racer wanted, so when Valentino began considering his move to 500s during 1999, he knew that only an NSR500 would do.

Of course, compared with a big, soft four-stroke, the NSR was never easy to ride, which is why Vale loved it so much. Given the choice, he would rather be racing 500s now, but smoky ol' two-strokes (nicknamed 'stinkwheels' by some) were consigned to history because they'd become marginalised by environmental concerns.

During its 17 years of GP racing the NSR won no fewer than 21 World Championships (ten riders' and 11 constructors').

SPECIFICATIONS

Honda NSR500 2001

ENGINE

Type: liquid-cooled V4 two-stroke, reed valve induction, with adjustable ignition, exhaust control, etc
Bore & stroke: 54 x 54.5mm
Displacement: 499cc
Fuel system: four 36mm magnesium Keihin carbs
Claimed output: 195 horsepower at 12,500rpm
Gearbox: six-speed, cassette type

CHASSIS

Frame type: dual beam aluminium
Tyres: Michelin
Wheels: 17in front, 16.5in rear
Front brake: 4-pot Brembo, twin 320mm carbon discs (dry), twin cast iron discs (wet)
Rear-brake: 2-pot Brembo, single 196mm disc
Front suspension: 47mm upside-down Showa, multi-adjustable
Rear suspension: Pro-link with Showa shock, multi-adjustable
Wheelbase: 1400mm
Length: 2010mm
Race weight: 131kg
Top speed: around 195mph

HONDA RC211V
2003

brembo
MICHELIN Pilot

Whichever way you look at it, Honda's RC211V looks squat, muscular and compact. Not an inch or an ounce wasted, this is the very pinnacle of the art and science of race-bike design.

STUDIO PHOTOS: TERUTAKA HOASHI/RIDERS CLUB

HONDA RC211V 2003

Honda's RC211V is probably about as close as you'll get to a perfect racing motorcycle. The V5 four-stroke ruled MotoGP's first two seasons, winning all but three of 32 races in 2002 and 2003, then Honda went and made their only mistake, somehow allowing Valentino to walk away and sign for Yamaha. The fact that they've had two lean years since Valentino defected reinforces that well-worn racetrack axiom: in motorcycle racing the man matters more than the machine.

Generally regarded as the most rider-friendly of the current generation of 250 horsepower MotoGP bikes, the RCV is the embodiment of Honda's five decades of motorcycle racing know-how. Squat, lean and muscular, the V5 was created to be a totally balanced motorcycle, so its engine, chassis and aerodynamics enhance each other for maximum all-round performance. It was the first race bike to properly realise the concept of 'mass centralisation', gathering as much weight as possible around the bike's centre of gravity for improved handling characteristics.

Honda designed its V5 motor for the same reason, with a relatively narrow 75.5 degree vee, because it would be compact. The engine's power characteristics are as cool, calm and collected as they can be, and if things do go wrong, there's a traction-control system that should prevent the rider losing control. So the RCV is a very manageable motorcycle, at least in relative terms, because no machine that can nudge 215mph is going to be a doddle to ride.

SPECIFICATIONS

Honda RC211V 2003

ENGINE

Type: liquid-cooled 20-valve 75.5 degree V5 four-stroke

Displacement: 990cc

Fuel system: PGM fuel injection

Claimed output: around 240 horsepower

Gearbox: six-speed, cassette type

CHASSIS

Frame type: dual beam aluminium

Tyres: Michelin

Wheels: 17in front, 16.5in rear

Front brake: 4-pot Brembo, twin carbon discs (dry), twin cast iron discs (wet)

Rear-brake: 2-pot Brembo, single disc

Front suspension: Upside-down Showa, multi-adjustable

Rear suspension: Pro-link with Showa shock, multi-adjustable

Wheelbase: 1440mm

Length: 2050mm

Race weight: over 145kg

Top speed: up to 215mph

YAMAHA YZR-M1
2004

46
2004
ÖHLINS
brembo

The M1 looks sharp, like a razorblade, and that's the way it handles too. Electronic trickery includes traction-control system and a full LCD dash with 15,000rpm tacho and inbuilt lap timer.

STUDIO PHOTOS:
TERUTAKA HOASHI/RIDERS CLUB

YAMAHA YZR-M1 2004

This is the bike that cemented Valentino's legend. When Vale quit Honda at the end of 2003, Yamaha's YZR-M1 was going through grim times, with just two wins from two seasons of MotoGP racing. By taking the 2004 title aboard the M1, Vale proved that he can win even when he doesn't have the best motorcycle beneath him. Prior to that – in 125s, 250s, 500s and MotoGP – he'd always had fully competitive machinery.

But Valentino did more than merely win the title for Yamaha. His special development abilities also helped the factory to drastically improve its M1. Vale's sensitivity to a bike's behaviour, his intelligence in understanding what's going on and his ability to communicate those thoughts and feelings to his engineers are as vital to his success as his instincts as a racer. The 2004 M1 was obviously not as good a motorcycle as Honda's RCV, but with a year of input from Valentino and his crew chief Jeremy Burgess, the 2005 M1 looked as good as the RCV, especially during the late stages of races, when bike behaviour is so crucial.

The Yamaha may seem less high-tech than the Honda, with its inline four motor (like the marque's R1 streetbike), but in fact it features some very clever technology. The M1's traction-control electronics inhibit wheelspin via engine and chassis sensors that monitor factors like lean angle and slip angle (via gyros and triple-axis sensors) to control wheelspin according to tyre wear and track conditions. ■

SPECIFICATIONS

Yamaha YZR-M1 2004

ENGINE

Type: liquid-cooled 16-valve inline four-cylinder four-stroke

Displacement: 990cc

Fuel system: fuel injection

Claimed output: over 240 horsepower

Gearbox: six-speed, cassette type

CHASSIS

Frame type: dual beam aluminium

Tyres: Michelin

Wheels: 16.5in front, 16.5in rear

Front brake: 4-pot Brembo, twin carbon discs (dry), twin cast iron discs (wet)

Rear-brake: 2-pot Brembo, single disc

Front suspension: Upside-down Showa, multi-adjustable

Rear suspension: Ohlins with rising-rate linkage, multi-adjustable

Race weight: over 145kg

Top speed: over 210mph

SETE GIBERNAU

'I've always said you can only ever aspire to being the best rider of your time. No-one can reasonably say who's the best ever because you can't compare riders from different eras. Right now Valentino's the best. He's always had great chances and he's always been able to profit from them, that's what makes him a champion. He's strongest because he wins in every area. To win races you've got to be like that – you've got to be talented, you've got to be mentally strong and you need everything working around you, like the team, plus you need some luck, too. Valentino's got all those things, he's winning and he deserves it.

'But don't ask me about him as a person, I'll only speak about him from a professional point of view, that's about it. I don't know why he's got a problem with me because I've never had a problem with him. I've always had a lot of respect for everyone on the grid, I just wish everyone shared that respect, because once you lose respect you lose everything.'

Gibernau is the grandson of Francesco Bulto, founder of the Bultaco marque (and one of Franco's artillery officers during Spain's civil war), so he comes from a biking family. He got into 250 GPs in the early '90s and graduated to 500s in '97, under the tutelage of former 500 champ Wayne Rainey. He used to be mates with Vale but they had a big falling out in 2004.

▲ If looks could kill. Gibernau ponders what Valentino's all about in a pre-race press conference at the 2005 Chinese GP.

GOLD AND GOOSE

'I don't know why he's got a problem with me'

ROSSI V GIBERNAU

Championship	Rossi	Gibernau
2004 MotoGP World Championship	Rossi 1st	Gibernau 2nd
2003 MotoGP World Championship	Rossi 1st	Gibernau 2nd
2002 MotoGP World Championship	Rossi 1st	Gibernau 16th
2001 500 World Championship	Rossi 1st	Gibernau 9th
2000 500 World Championship	Rossi 2nd	Gibernau 15th

◀ Best mates or sworn rivals, Vale and Gibernau have always raced each other hard. This is Brno 2003, with Troy Bayliss in the mix.

GOLD AND GOOSE

LORIS CAPIROSSI

'I've always been friendly with Valentino because he's a good guy, though maybe it's easy to be friends with me because I'm a quiet man. I've known him since 1990, because I knew his father. I'd just started doing GPs and he had started minimoto. Every time he came to a bike show or some other event he used to really break my balls – he would come to me and say "please give me a helmet", or "please give me a boot", or "give me a set of leathers"... always. Fucking hell! I remember so well Brno '93, when he came to watch the GP and he slept in my motorhome, he was just a kid then.

'He's really strong and he loves to fight. In 1999 we had a lot of races together, lots of overtaking but always fair, we would look at each other during the race and smile, we had a lot of fun. Sometimes when I beat him he wasn't happy, but after ten minutes he'd be okay. I don't think it's his riding style that makes the difference. At this level everyone is a very good rider, it's his brain that makes the difference, he's very clever.'

Capirossi was GP racing's first teenage superstar. He won the 1990 125 world title aged 17, and he's still the sport's youngest world champ. He raced Rossi in the 1998 and '99 250 championships, then in the 500 and MotoGP series.

▲ When he was a kid Vale was a fan of teenage 125 champ Capirossi. They've remained good mates ever since.

GOLD AND GOOSE

ROSSI RIVALS

The men who've given him the hardest time in 125s, 250s, 500s and MotoGP

▼ Valentino and Capirossi had some of their best battles in the 1999 250 World Championship, when they rode for Aprilia and Honda. Vale beat Capirossi here in Germany and for the title.

GOLD AND GOOSE

ROSSI V CAPIROSSI

2004 MotoGP World Championship
Rossi 1st Capirossi 9th

2003 MotoGP World Championship
Rossi 1st Capirossi 4th

2002 MotoGP World Championship
Rossi 1st Capirossi 8th

2001 500 World Championship
Rossi 1st Capirossi 3rd

2000 500 World Championship
Rossi 2nd Capirossi 7th

1999 250 World Championship
Rossi 1st Capirossi 3rd

1998 250 World Championship
Rossi 2nd Capirossi 1st

◀ Two people with not much to say to each other – the Roman Emperor and the Doctor suffer the agony of yet another press conference.
GOLD AND GOOSE

ROSSI V BIAGGI	
2004 MotoGP World Championship	
Rossi 1st	Biaggi 3rd
2003 MotoGP World Championship	
Rossi 1st	Biaggi 3rd
2002 MotoGP World Championship	
Rossi 1st	Biaggi 2nd
2001 500 World Championship	
Rossi 1st	Biaggi 2nd
2000 500 World Championship	
Rossi 2nd	Biaggi 3rd

MAX BIAGGI

'I've never been friends with him. I just go my own way, at least I don't pretend to be his friend like some guys, which is just theatre, like fake friends. I always say it's impossible to have a friendship with a rival. I'm true, whatever I say, I just give my opinion and that's me. If you like me, okay, if you don't like me, okay, but at least I'm true.

'What do I think about his riding technique? I don't see anything very particular, but he's the man to beat. When I see him it just seems he works very well with the package. In 2001 I was the only one who could fight with him. He was very good on the brakes but I think that was because the Honda was always so strong on braking, while we had some front-end problems with the Yamaha. Even so, we gave 100 per cent to be fastest and sometimes we were.'

The self-styled Roman Emperor was Rossi's first big, bad rival, as opposed to the mates he'd played with in 125s and 250s. The two hated each other's guts even before they raced each other. After their infamous punch-up in 2001 the imperious Biaggi explained away a graze on his face with the immortal words: 'A mosquito bit me.'

▼ Through most of their rivalry, Rossi has generally had the best bike. This is Brno 2002, which Biaggi won on the Yamaha M1. That's the late Daijiro Kato in the background.
GOLD AND GOOSE

NOBBY UEDA

'I first knew Rossi when he was 11, because I lived only one kilometre from him in Italy. Some nights we would race each other at minimoto, I wasn't as good as him!

'His riding style was very wild when he first came to GPs, he crashed many times. I think he was studying the limit and how he could control his machine. By '97 it was very difficult to beat him. His riding skill is about controlling his weight on the bike – through the footpegs, the seat, the tank, the handlebars. He moves so well, it's like he's dancing on the bike. This allows him to move traction between the front and rear tyres, depending where he is in the corner, and it also helps turn the bike, especially when the tyres are finished. He can find side grip especially at the end of races by shifting backwards and pushing on the outside footpeg to put weight on the rear tyre. He was fun to race, he never cut me up, but I knew I couldn't play with him, so I just gave gas all the time. Frankly speaking, I feel sorry for him now, his life is too busy – too many fans come to see him, too many journalists, too many cameramen.'

Ever-smiling Ueda led the new wave of Japanese riders to GPs in the early '90s. Second in the '94 and '97 125 World Championships, he kept racing until 2002.

▼ Vale and Nobby got on because they shared a similar attitude to racing – why do it unless you're having fun? Ueda's just been beaten by Vale at the '97 Spanish GP but he's still grinning like crazy.
GOLD AND GOOSE

▲ Tucked in to squeeze every mile an hour out of their puny 125s, Rossi and Ueda play the slipstream game at Rio '97. Rossi won by a few yards.
GOLD AND GOOSE

ROSSI V UEDA

1997 125 World Championship
Rossi 1st Ueda 2nd

1996 125 World Championship
Rossi 9th Ueda 7th

'It's like he's dancing on the bike'

Ueda

GAULOISES
GAULOISES
YAMAHA
MOTUL
MICHELIN

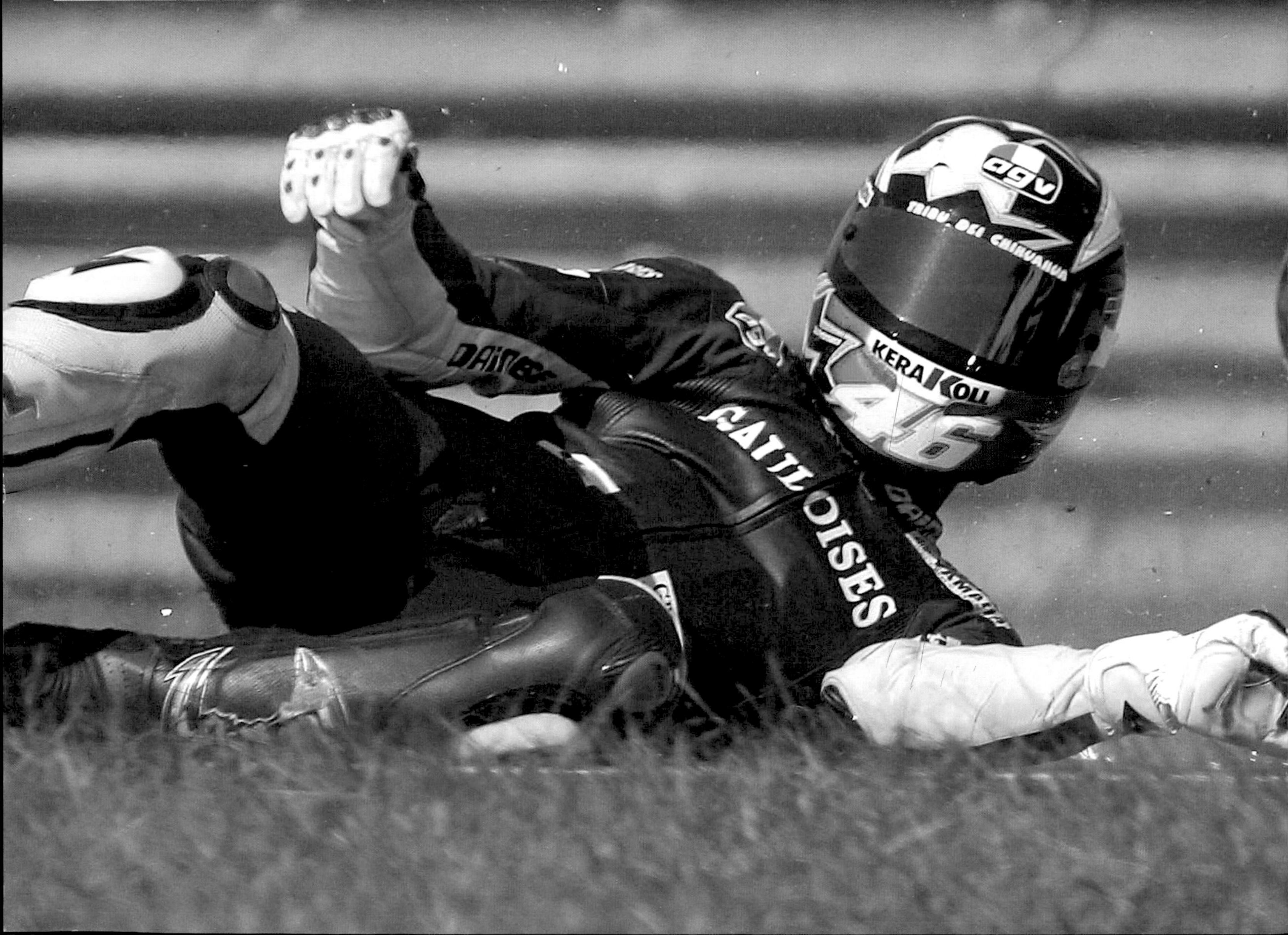

Because even a genius gets it wrong now and again

ROSSI DOWN

This is the moment Vale thought he'd thrown away the 2004 World Championship. Struggling to stay with the faster Hondas at Rio, he finally pushed his M1 beyond the brink. But he learned plenty from this crash: when the bike ain't right, it's better to score a few points than none.

KEULEMANS

'In my mind I try to ride fast, then make mistake. I need this for go faster, is a system'

▲ Sitting on his arse again – Valentino crashed way too many times during his debut GP season in '96. As his team boss Giampiero Sacchi recalls: 'Many came from Vale just not thinking; the tyres: cold! Give gas: crash!'

GOLD AND GOOSE

► Racers always have to learn the hard way – Vale gets ejected from his Honda NSR while battling with Garry McCoy and Kenny Roberts Junior (2) at Sepang, April 2000. This was his second 500 GP and his second tumble.

BARSHON

▼ Honda's RCV is such a rider-friendly tool that Vale only crashed it a few times. This minor tumble, during practice for the 2003 German GP, was his first in more than a year and over 9000 miles of riding.

GOLD AND GOOSE

▲ The end of Valentino's Hawaiian dream. Leaving his own wake on the soaking Mugello track, Vale crashes out of the 2001 Italian GP. He'd been trying too hard to catch the leaders.

GPMP

◀ Even after Vale had mastered 500s, the NSR could still creep up and bite him when he was least expecting it. He survived this get-off at Phillip Island in 2001 to secure the 500 title the following day.

MILAGRO

▲ Vale makes an ignominious exit, eating the Le Mans dirt during morning warm-up for the 2004 French GP. Struggling with handling problems, he recovered to finish fourth.

MILAGRO

▲ Valentino reckons this tumble marks his career's lowest ebb. Despite a crash-ridden start to his debut 250 season in '98, he still had a chance of the title, until this crash, just four corners into the Czech GP.

GOLD AND GOOSE

'60s LEGEND
GIACOMO AGOSTINI

'Mother nature gives you this kind of talent. His dad rode for my team once – he wasn't so bad but not like his son. He started racing as a young boy, just doing what he liked doing, playing around, and now he's doing the same but in a different way. He has everything you need to win – courage, sensitivity with the bike, and so on.

'He's fantastic and he's the best rider out there. He proved that to everybody by changing factories. But it's stupid to ask if he's the best ever. How can you say he's better than Mike Hailwood? To compare them is impossible.'

Ago is the most successful rider of all, with 15 world titles and more than 120 GP wins. He ruled the '60s and kept winning into the '70s. The Italian heartthrob also starred in some movies, then went into team management.

'70s LEGEND
KING KENNY ROBERTS

'The biggest problem with beating Valentino is that he doesn't mind getting beat. To be a good winner you've got to be a good loser. Some days he'll take third, if there's any chance of overcooking it. What keeps him winning is the fact that he loves it all: racing, practice, testing. But is he the greatest? I don't know, I don't think you can classify anyone like that.

'He rides a bit too close to the limit sometimes, but if he can get away with it, more power to him. It's just his natural ability coming through more than thinking about it: "Okay, I'm going to win this".'

King Kenny Roberts was the first American to win the 500 World Championship, in 1978, using tail-sliding dirt track techniques. He won a hat trick of titles, became a team manager and now builds his own MotoGP bikes.

'Mother nature gives you this kind of talent'

Giacomo Agostini

▼ Charm offensive: 60s Italian heartthrob Giacomo Agostini chats to 21st century heartthrob Vale on the grid at Mugello, 2003.
KEULEMANS

▶ Eddie Lawson was a smooth, deep-thinking rider, just like Valentino.
GOLD AND GOOSE

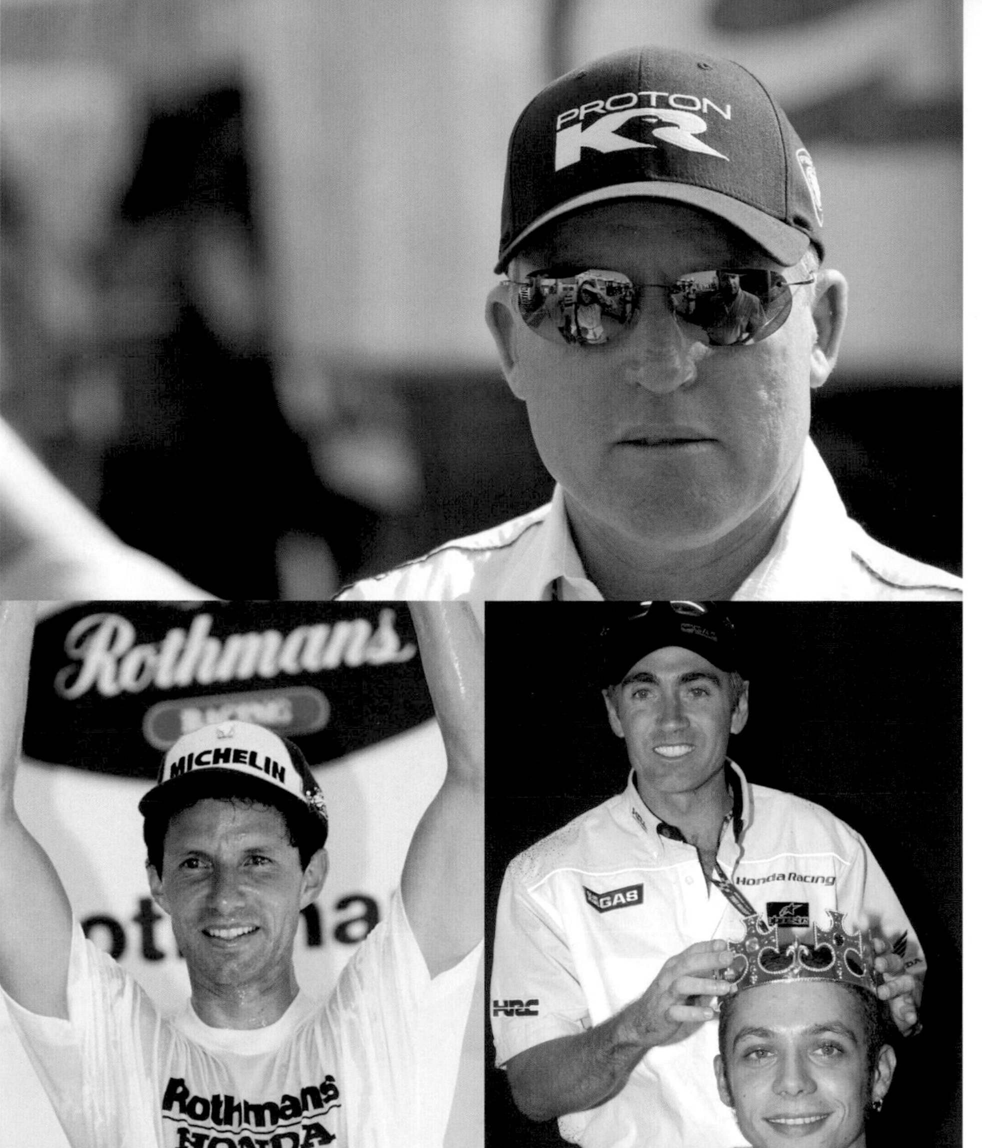

◀ No-one understands bike racing and bike riding like King Kenny does.
GOLD AND GOOSE

▼ The king is dead, long live the king! Mick Doohan hadn't been long gone from GPs before a worthy successor to his crown was found.
MILAGRO

ROSSI VERSUS HISTORY

Is he the greatest racer ever? The legends of the '60s, '70s, '80s and '90s decide…

'80s LEGEND EDDIE LAWSON

'He could be the best ever but it's hard to compare different times. I'm impressed by the guy because he goes fast all the time. He just seems to have the combination of everything where he can ride fast when it's hot, when it's cold, when he doesn't like the track, when it's raining... He's always fast, whereas the other guys seem like they're "I'm from Spain, so I'll go fast when I'm in Spain". Plus he thinks about stuff and he's dedicated.

'I like the way he rides. He's in control, he doesn't want the bike sliding or wobbling because you go fast with momentum, not by being on the ragged edge.'

Four-time 500 champ Lawson was the first man to win consecutive 500 titles on different bikes, in 1988/1989, quitting Yamaha for Honda. 'Steady Eddie' was a thinking man's racer, known for smooth riding.

'90s LEGEND MICK DOOHAN

'Valentino is immensely talented as far as riding a motorcycle goes, but he also has the capacity to think his way through a race. He doesn't get too flustered, he gets going when he needs to, then pulls off the fastest lap on the last lap to win. But if it's the last lap and he's going to finish second, that's where he finishes, he doesn't pitch it down the road. He's well ahead of the bike while the other guys are struggling to keep up with them. So, yes, he's an extremely talented rider, but is he more talented than Eddie Lawson or Kenny Roberts? I don't know, I don't think I can really answer that one.'

Doohan ruled the '90s, winning five back-to-back 500 crowns. After he retired Rossi inherited his pit crew. As HRC general manager, Doohan offered advice to Rossi during his first years on big bikes.

▲ Like a kid at a car show, Valentino checks out Schumi's Ferrari at the 2005 Australian F1 GP. During this visit, while taking some holiday from pre-season tests at Phillip Island, Vale and his gang arranged a secret try-out at Ferrari's test track.

GOSLING

► With no F1-spec driving kit of his own, Vale tested the Ferrari in Schumi's helmet and suit. The outing displeased all his MotoGP backers: Yamaha because it's part-owned by Ferrari's F1 rival Toyota, Gauloises because Ferrari is backed by Marlboro, and Michelin because Schumacher uses Bridgestones.

COLOMBO

◄ Keeping his date with destiny, Vale starts his first WRC event, the Rally of Great Britain, November 2002. He crashed out on the first stage but don't be surprised if he goes rallying after bikes – he prefers it to F1.
DOUBLE RED

AUTO ROSSI

Valentino started his racing career on four wheels and will probably end it on four wheels…

◄ Schumi told Vale he was impressed by the bike champ's efforts but declined an offer to try out the M1. Wimp! Meanwhile Ferrari president Luca di Montezemolo insisted that he's ready to give Rossi a drive any time: 'There will always be an open door for him at Ferrari'.
COLOMBO

PREMIER-CLASS WINS [MODERN ERA: 1975-2005]

	RIDER	STARTS	WINS	WINNING %
1	Valentino Rossi	87	48	55%
2	Mick Doohan	137	54	39%
3	Kenny Roberts (Snr)	58	22	38%
4	Freddie Spencer	62	20	32%
5	Wayne Rainey	83	24	29%
6	Eddie Lawson	127	31	24%
7	Kevin Schwantz	104	25	24%
8	Barry Sheene	98	19	19%
9	Wayne Gardner	102	18	18%
10	Pat Hennen	24	3	13%

PREMIER-CLASS WINS [ALL GPs: 1949-2005]

	RIDER	STARTS	WINS	WINNING %
1	John Surtees	34	22	65%
2	Giacomo Agostini	119	68	57%
3	Mike Hailwood	65	37	57%
4	Valentino Rossi	87	48	55%
5	Geoff Duke	55	22	40%
6	Mick Doohan	137	54	39%
7	Kenny Roberts (Snr)	58	22	38%
8	Wayne Rainey	83	24	29%
9	Eddie Lawson	127	31	24%
10	Kevin Schwantz	104	25	24%

PREMIER-CLASS PODIUMS [MODERN ERA: 1975-2005]

	RIDER	STARTS	PODIUMS	PODIUM %
1	Valentino Rossi	87	72	83%
2	Wayne Rainey	83	64	77%
3	Mick Doohan	137	95	69%
4	Kenny Roberts (Snr)	58	39	67%
5	Eddie Lawson	127	78	61%
6	Wayne Gardner	102	52	51%
7	Freddie Spencer	62	31	50%
8	Pat Hennen	24	12	50%
9	Kevin Schwantz	104	51	49%
10	Max Biaggi	117	56	48%

PREMIER-CLASS PODIUMS [ALL GPs: 1949-2005]

	RIDER	STARTS	PODIUMS	PODIUM %
1	Valentino Rossi	87	72	83%
2	Wayne Rainey	83	64	77%
3	Giacomo Agostini	119	88	74%
4	Mike Hailwood	65	48	74%
5	John Surtees	34	24	71%
6	Mick Doohan	137	95	69%
7	Kenny Roberts (Snr)	58	39	67%
8	Eddie Lawson	127	78	61%
9	Geoff Duke	55	32	58%
10	Kevin Schwantz	104	51	49%

PREMIER-CLASS POLES [MODERN ERA: 1975-2005]

	RIDER	STARTS	POLES	POLE %
1	Mick Doohan	137	58	42%
2	Freddie Spencer	62	26	42%
3	Valentino Rossi	87	29	33%
4	Johnny Cecotto	34	11	32%
5	Kenny Roberts (Snr)	58	18	31%
6	Kevin Schwantz	104	29	28%
7	Max Biaggi	117	23	20%
8	Wayne Gardner	102	19	19%
9	Barry Sheene	98	18	18%
10	Wayne Rainey	83	15	18%

ANORAKS' CORNER

■ Valentino has never missed a GP since he made his debut in Malaysia in March 1996. The US GP in July 2005 was thus his 148th consecutive GP race ■ When he won the 2001 500 world title he became only the third rider to win crowns in three different classes, after Phil Read (125, 250 and 500) and Mike Hailwood (250, 350 and 500) ■ Valentino is the only rider to have won World Championships in four classes: 125, 250, 500 and MotoGP ■ Vale and Giacomo Agostini are the only two riders to have won premier-class world titles with both two-stroke and four-stroke machinery ■ His win at the 2004 season-opening GP made him the first rider to take back-to-back premier-class victories riding different makes of bike ■ In 2004 he became the second rider to win back-to-back premier-class titles on different makes of machinery. Eddie Lawson was the first, winning on a Yamaha in 1988 and a Honda in 1989 ■ Valentino is the only rider to have scored five consecutive premier-class victories on a Yamaha ■ In 2004 he scored nine victories, the highest number of wins ever achieved by a premier-class Yamaha rider in a single season ■ He is the only rider in history to have won five or more consecutive premier-class victories on two different makes of bike ■ He holds the record for consecutive premier-class podiums, scoring 23 successive top-three results finishes from Portugal 2002 to South Africa 2004. Agostini was the previous record holder with 22 top-threes during 1967, 1968 and 1969 ■ Valentino had the honour of scoring Honda's 500th GP victory when he won the Japanese 500 GP in April 2001 ■ He became the youngest-ever rider to win the 250 World Championship when he took the title in 1999 ■ Valentino finished on the podium at all 16 GPs in 2003, a record number of podiums for a single season

MotoGP RESULTS

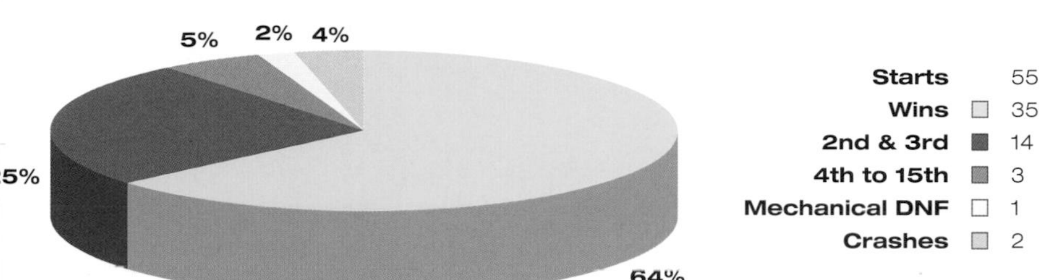

500 RESULTS

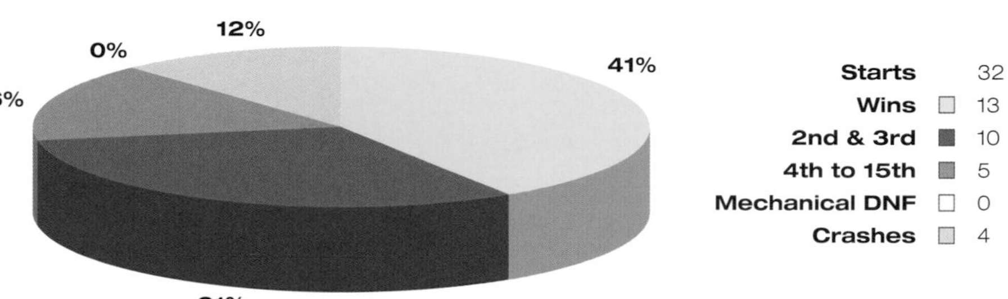

250 RESULTS

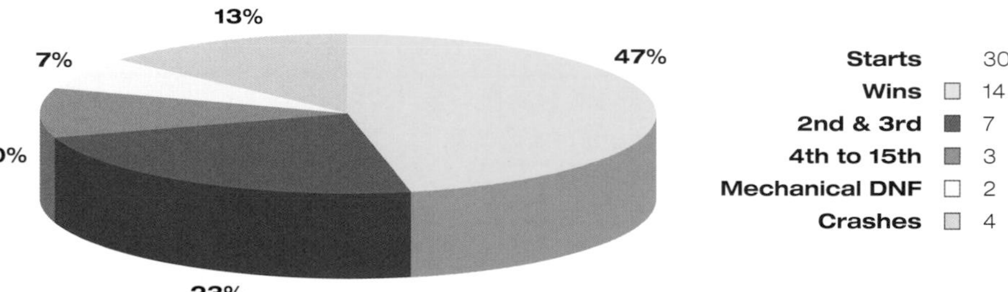

125 RESULTS

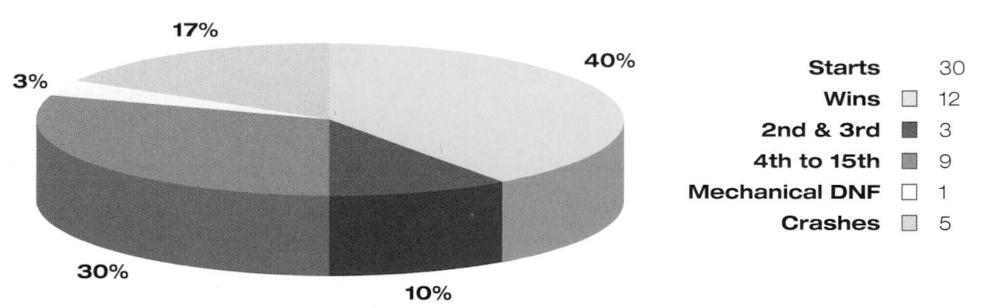

COMBINED RESULTS (ALL CLASSES)

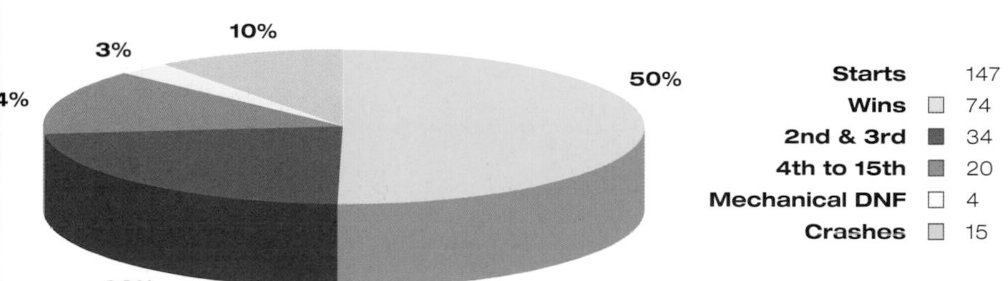

ROSSI BY NUMBERS

Awesome statistics that prove the man's genius

ALL STATISTICS COMPILED BY DR MARTIN RAINES, JULY 2005

November 2002: Rossi has just quit Honda after falling out with bearded HRC boss Kohji Nakajima. Time to ambush him down a dark alley, with a little help from JB.

Cartoon genius Sprocket reminds us that

February 2004: The general consensus is that Valentino will need extra-large balls to win the world title on the Yamaha. Enter Yamaha boss Davide Brivio…

March 2005: Honda lines up seven RCV riders to take on 'Not Slow White' Rossi. From left: Hayden, Gibernau, Barros, Melandri, Biaggi, Bayliss and Tamada.

at the end of the day, it's all a bit of a laugh....

June 2004: Vale reckons Gibernau is a bit of a Narcissus, which is why he calls him 'Hollywood' – hence this handy little seat-mounted mirror set.

ROSSI RESULTS

1996 125 World Championship: 9th. Bike: AGV Aprilia RS125R – March 31, Malaysian GP, Shah Alam: 13th/6th. April 7, Indonesian GP, Sentul: 18th/11th. April 21, Japanese GP, Suzuka: 10th/11th. May 12, Spanish GP, Jerez: 7th/4th. May 26, Italian GP, Mugello: 8th/4th. June 9, French GP, Paul Ricard: 13th/DNF, crash, FL. June 29, Dutch GP, Assen: 8th/DNF, crash. July 7, German GP, Nürburgring: 4th/5th July 21, British GP, Donington Park: 9th/DNF, mech. August 4, Austrian GP, A1-Ring: 3rd/3rd. August 18, Czech GP, Brno: pole/1st. September 9, City of Imola GP, Imola: 2nd/5th, FL. September 15, Catalan GP, Catalunya: 5th/DNF, crash. October 6, Rio GP, Jacarepagua: 11th/DNF, crash. October 20, Australian GP, Eastern Creek: 12th/14th. 1997 125 World Championship: 1st. Bike: Nastro Azzurro Aprilia RS125R – April 13, Malaysian GP, Shah Alam: pole/1st, FL. April 20, Japanese GP, Suzuka: 7th/DNF, crash. May 4, Spanish GP, Jerez: 6th/1st, FL. May 18, Italian GP, Mugello: 3rd/1st. June 1, Austrian GP, A1-Ring: 2nd/2nd, FL. June 8, French GP, Paul Ricard: 3rd/1st. June 28, Dutch GP, Assen: pole/1st. July 6 City of Imola GP, Imola: pole/1st, FL. July 20, German GP, Nürburgring : pole/1st. August 3, Rio GP, Jacarepagua: 2nd/1st, FL. August 17, British GP, Donington Park: 4th/1st, FL. August 31, Czech GP, Brno: 3rd/3rd. September 14, Catalan GP, Catalunya: 4th/1st. September 29, Indonesian GP, Sentul: 4th/1st, FL. October 5, Australian GP, Phillip Island: 3rd/6th. **1998 250 World Championship: 2nd. Bike: Nastro Azzurro Aprilia RSW250 – April 5, Japanese GP, Suzuka: 7th/DNF, mech. April 19, Malaysian GP, Johor: 2nd/DNF, crash, FL. May 3, Spanish GP, Jerez: 3rd/2nd. May 17, Italian GP, Mugello: 4th/2nd. May 31, French GP, Paul Ricard: 3rd/2nd. June 14, Madrid GP, Jarama: 4th/DNF, crash. June 27, Dutch GP, Assen: 3rd/1st. July 5, British GP, Donington Park: 2nd/DNF, crash. July 19, German GP, Sachsenring: 4th/3rd. August 23, Czech GP, Brno: 2nd/DNF, crash. September 6, City of Imola GP, Imola: 5th/1st. September 20, Catalan GP, Catalunya: 2nd/1st, FL. October 4, Australian GP, Phillip Island: 2nd/1st. October 25, Argentine GP, Buenos Aires: 3rd/1st, FL** 1999 250 World Championship: 1st. Bike: Nastro Azzurro Aprilia RSW250 – April 18, Malaysian GP, Sepang : pole/5th. April 25, Japanese GP, Motegi: 11th/7th. May 9, Spanish GP, Jerez: 3rd/1st. May 23, French GP, Paul Ricard: pole/DNF, mech, FL. June 6, Italian GP, Mugello: 6th/1st, FL. June 20, Catalan GP, Catalunya: 2nd/1st, FL. June 26, Dutch GP, Assen: pole/2nd, FL. July 4, British GP, Donington Park: 3rd/1st. July 18, German GP, Sachsenring: pole/1st. August 28, Czech GP, Brno: 3rd/1st, FL. September 5, City of Imola GP, Imola: 3rd/2nd. September 19, Valencia GP, Valencia: 4th/8th. October 3, Australian GP, Phillip Island: 7th/1st, FL. October 10, South African GP, Welkom: 6th/1st, FL. October 24, Rio GP, Jacarepagua: 2nd/1st, FL. October 31, Argentine GP, Buenos Aires: pole/3rd. **2000 500 World Championship: 2nd. Bike: Nastro Azzurro Honda NSR500 – March 19, South African GP, Welkom: 5th/DNF, crash, FL. April 2, Malaysian GP, Sepang: 7th/DNF, crash. April 9, Japanese GP, Suzuka: 13th/11th. April 30, Spanish GP, Jerez: 2nd/3rd. April 14, French GP, Le Mans: 10th/3rd, FL. May 28, Italian GP, Mugello: 3rd/DNF, crash. June 11: Catalan GP, Catalunya: 9th/3rd. June 24, Dutch GP, Assen: 6th/6th. July 9, British GP, Donington Park: 4th/1st. July 23, German GP, Sachsenring: 6th/2nd. August 20, Czech GP, Brno: 5th/2nd. September 3, Portuguese GP, Estoril: 12th/3rd, FL. September 17, Valencia GP, Valencia: 5th/DNF, crash. October 7, Rio GP, Jacarepagua: 4th/1st, FL.October 15, Pacific GP, Motegi: 5th/2nd, FL. October 29, Australian GP, Phillip Island: 8th/3rd.** 2001 500 World Championship: 1st. Bike: Nastro Azzurro Honda NSR500 – April 8, Japanese GP, Suzuka: 7th/1st. April 22, South African GP, Welkom: pole/1st, FL. May 6, Spanish GP, Jerez: pole/1st, FL. May 20, French GP, Le Mans: 3rd/3rd. June 3, Italian GP, Mugello: pole/DNF, crash, FL. June 17, Catalan GP, Catalunya: pole/1st, FL. June 30, Dutch GP, Assen: 3rd/2nd, FL. July 8, British GP, Donington Park: 11th/1st, FL. July 22, German GP, Sachsenring: 11th/7th. August 26, Czech GP, Brno: 2nd/1st, FL. September 9, Portuguese GP, Estoril: 3rd/1st. September 23, Valencia GP, Valencia: 2nd/11th. October 7, Pacific GP, Motegi: 4th/1st, FL. October 14, Australian GP, Phillip Island: 2nd/1st. October 21, Malaysian GP, Sepang: 2nd/1st, FL. November 3, Rio GP, Jacarepagua: 5th/1st,FL. **2002 MotoGP World Championship: 1st. Bike: Repsol Honda RC211V – April 7, Japanese GP, Suzuka: pole/1st, FL. April 21, South African GP, Welkom: pole/2nd. May 5, Spanish GP, Jerez: pole/1st, FL. May 19, French GP, Le Mans: pole/1st, FL. June 2, Italian GP, Mugello: pole/1st. June 16, Catalan GP, Catalunya: 4th/1st, FL. June 29, Dutch TT, Assen: pole/1st, FL. July 14, British GP, Donington Park: pole/1st, FL. July 21, German GP, Sachsenring: 6th/1st, FL. August 25, Czech GP, Brno: 3rd/DNF, mech. September 8, Portuguese GP, Estoril: 3rd/1st, FL. September 21, Rio GP, Jacarepagua: 2nd/1st. October 6, Pacific GP, Motegi: 6th/2nd. October 31, Malaysian GP, Sepang: 8th/2nd. October 20, Australian GP, Phillip Island: 7th/1st, FL. November 3, Valencia GP, Valencia: 6th/2nd.** 2003 MotoGP World Championship: 1st. Bike: Repsol Honda RC211V – April 6, Japanese GP, Suzuka: pole/1st, FL. April 27, South African GP, Welkom: 2nd/2nd, FL. May 11, Spanish GP, Jerez: 5th/1st, FL. May 25, French GP, Le Mans: pole/2nd. June 8, Italian GP, Mugello: pole/1st. June 15, Catalan GP, Catalunya: pole/2nd, FL. June 28, Dutch TT, Assen: 3rd/3rd. July 13, British GP, Donington Park: 4th/3rd, FL. July 27, German GP, Sachsenring: 4th/2nd. August 17, Czech GP, Brno: pole/1st, FL. September 7, Portuguese GP, Estoril: 3rd/1st, FL. September 20, Rio GP, Jacarepagua: pole/1st. October 5, Pacific GP, Motegi: 3rd/2nd, FL. October 12, Malaysian GP, Sepang: pole/1st, FL. October 19, Australian GP, Phillip Island: pole/1st, FL. November 2, Valencia GP, Valencia: pole/1st, FL. **2004 MotoGP World Championship: 1st. Bike: Gauloises Yamaha YZR-M1 – April 18, South African GP, Welkom: pole/1st. May 2, Spanish GP, Jerez: pole/4th. May 16, French GP, Le Mans: 4th/4th. June 6, Italian GP, Mugello: 3rd/1st. June 13, Catalan GP, Catalunya: 2nd/1st. June 26, Dutch TT, Assen: pole/1st, FL. July 4, Rio GP, Jacarepagua: 8th/DNF, crash. July 18, German GP, Sachsenring: 2nd/4th. July 25, British GP, Donington Park: pole/1st. August 22, Czech GP, Brno: 3rd/2nd. September 5, Portuguese GP, Estoril: 2nd/1st, FL. September 9, Japanese GP, Motegi: 3rd/2nd. October 2, Qatar GP, Losail: 8th/DNF, crash. October 10, Malaysian GP, Sepang: pole/1st, FL. October 17, Australian GP, Phillip Island: 2nd/1st. October 31, Valencia GP, Valencia: 3rd/1st.** 2005 MotoGP World Championship. Bike: Gauloises Yamaha YZR-M1 – April 10, Spanish GP, Jerez: 1st/1st, FL. April 17, Portuguese GP, Estoril: 4th/2nd. May 1, Chinese GP, Shanghai: 6th/1st. May 15, French GP, Le Mans: 1st/1st, FL. June 5, Italian GP, Mugello: 1st/1st. June 12, Catalan GP, Catalunya: 3rd/1st, FL. June 25, Dutch TT, Assen: pole/1st. FL. And so on and so forth… ■

Grid/race results. FL = fastest lap.
DNF = did not finish. Mech = machine failure.